28 Days
to
Knowing
God

28 Days
to
Knowing
God

DAVE EARLEY

BARBOUR BOOKS
An Imprint of Barbour Publishing, Inc.

This book is well suited to use by small groups. Please see page 185 for more information.

© 2019 by Dave Earley

ISBN 978-1-64352-004-9

Published by Barbour Books, an imprint of Barbour Publishing, Inc., 1810 Barbour Drive, Uhrichsville, Ohio 44683, www.barbourbooks.com

Our mission is to inspire the world with the life-changing message of the Bible.

 Member of the
Evangelical Christian
Publishers Association

Printed in the United States of America.

Contents

"THEO 311"

I felt lost.

Even though I was just a recent Christian and a brand-new college freshman, a series of circumstances led me into THEO 311, an upper-level theology class. Surrounded by a group of confident upperclassmen who had been studying religion for several years, I felt out of my depth.

But, thankfully, I realized that this class wasn't just abstract theories. Instead, it was about knowing God. That was exactly what I longed for and needed. During the next two months, as our class ventured into the doctrine of God, the truth I was learning about Him blew my mind, built my faith, and blessed my life. Now, even though I have two doctorate degrees, I can say that out of the ninety-seven different courses I took in college and graduate school, THEO 311 was the most important and influential. Let me tell you why.

Learning about God Blew My Mind

I learned that God is bigger and better than I had ever thought or imagined. Every day as I read the assignments, listened to the lectures, and studied the scriptures, I strained to have my little brain comprehend all the big and amazing truths I was learning about God.

I discovered that He is greater than anything or anyone else, anywhere, ever. He is infinite, incomprehensible, indescribable, and undeniable. He is self-sufficient and self-existent. In all the universe, He alone is ageless and eternal. He dwells outside the realm of space and time. He possesses unlimited knowledge, as well as incomparable power, authority, and strength.

Yet God is not merely bigger than anyone or anything else,

He is also *better*. He alone possesses perfect holiness and perfect love. He has unlimited resources of grace and mercy. He is uniquely and absolutely just, righteous, and true. He is faithful, wise, compassionate, kind, and patient.

Learning about God Built My Faith

The effectiveness of our faith is not based on how much we possess, but rather on what we put our faith in. It is possible to have great faith in something that will let us down.

When I was very young and rather poor, I pulled my meager but hard-earned money together to buy a Reliant K car. *Consumer Reports* had rated it very highly. The salesman told me it was a great car. I trusted the car and believed with all my heart that it would give me years of safe, reliable service.

Ha!

It was a piece of junk, one that within a few years would break down at the worst, most inopportune moments. When the Reliant K almost failed to get my very pregnant wife to the hospital to deliver our first baby, I knew it had to go. That car proved to be an unworthy object of faith.

I had few expectations of my next car, a used Honda Accord. But no matter how much faith I had, this car ran well. Over time, I put many carefree miles on that Honda, and I have been buying Accords ever since. Though I didn't start with much faith in it, this car proved to be a worthy object of my faith.

As I learned more about God, I discovered that He is a worthy object of faith. And my faith increased. I had a new level of trust and a greater depth of reliance upon Him.

Learning about God Blessed My Life

As I learned more about God, my life positively transformed. I prayed more often and more effectively. I worried less often and about fewer things. I slept better. I lost my fear about the future. I had more strength to face trials and resist temptation. It was easier to trust God with my finances. I found a purpose and passion for living. I had more confidence in sharing my faith. I ministered to believers with greater wisdom.

Learning about God reduced many of the stresses of life:

- Why not trust my future to the One who is already in the future?
- Why not depend upon a good and all-powerful Father who loves me?
- Why not trust the Bible, since it is the result of the breath of God?
- Why be consumed with my problems when God is infinitely bigger than they are?
- Why worry about what other people think when God's opinion is the only one that counts—and He loves me unconditionally?
- Why not pray with expectancy since God is able?

But there was even more than that.

God went from being a distant Being I believed in to the most important Person in my life, every day of my life—not just on Sundays. I began to set aside time over lunch to read His Word and talk with Him about every aspect of my life: the good, the bad, and the ugly. Those daily, noon-time appointments with God marked me.

Why Get to Know God?

God created you to know Him. Knowing Him transforms you into the person He created you to be. . .the person you always wanted to be. I encourage you to invest the next 28 days in getting to know God. The Bible offers many important reasons for doing that.

Knowing God is the basis of eternal life

In John 17, Jesus prayed for Himself, His disciples, and everyone who would ever believe in Him. In this "high priestly prayer," as theologians call it, Jesus made an astounding little statement:

"Now this is eternal life: that they know you, the only true God, and Jesus Christ, whom you have sent."
John 17:3

Jesus declared that "eternal life" is not something that starts after a Christian dies. Eternal life refers to a higher quality of life here and now. It speaks of a personal relationship of knowing God while we walk this earth. The moment you meet God through salvation, eternal life begins. The more you get to know and experience God, the more this life grows.

KNOWING GOD INCREASES OUR INNER STRENGTH, ENERGY, AND ENDURANCE

Near the end of his powerful Old Testament book, the prophet Daniel discussed the rise of the antichrist, an evil world ruler of the end times. Quoting the angel man sent to him from God, Daniel wrote that there is a certain type of person who gains spiritual strength and is able to resist the enemy—the person who knows God:

> *"The people who know their God shall be strong, and carry out great exploits."*
> DANIEL 11:32 NKJV

KNOWING GOD PROVIDES DIVINE PROTECTION

The knowledge of God is so central to God's people that they are hopeless without it. God said,

> *"My people are being destroyed because they don't know me."*
> HOSEA 4:6 NLT

The best way to prepare and protect yourself is to make sure that you are personally and passionately pursuing the Lord.

KNOWING GOD PLEASES HIM AND BRINGS YOU GREAT FULFILLMENT

What gives God deep delight? Our efforts to know Him.

> *"For I desire mercy and not sacrifice, and the knowledge of God more than burnt offerings."*
> HOSEA 6:6 NKJV

Our purpose is to *know God*. Therefore, it makes sense that we will be fulfilled only to the extent that we pursue that purpose.

> *Thus says the LORD: "Let not the wise man glory in his wisdom, let not the mighty man glory in his might, nor let the rich man glory in his riches; but let him who glories glory in this, that he understands and knows Me, that I am the LORD, exercising lovingkindness, judgment, and righteousness in the earth. For in these I delight," says the LORD.*
> JEREMIAH 9:23–24 NKJV

KNOWING GOD IS THE SUPREME PURSUIT.

The apostle Paul was an up-and-coming, big-time Jewish religious leader on the verge of stardom. He had proudly built a religion based on his own righteousness and religious achievements—including the persecution of people who followed Jesus, who is God's Son and yet also one with the Father. As a strict monotheist, Paul couldn't imagine that God had a son.

But then Jesus wonderfully wrecked his life. From that moment on, Paul said that he had one primary pursuit that trumped everything else in his life—to know Christ! He was willing to turn his back on everything else to know Jesus:

> *Yes, everything else is worthless when compared with the infinite value of knowing Christ Jesus my Lord. For his sake I have discarded everything else, counting it all as garbage, so that I could gain Christ. . . . I want to know Christ.*
> PHILIPPIANS 3:8–10 NLT

What It Means to "Know God"

When the Bible speaks of "knowing" something, the writers were careful to distinguish between knowing *about* something and knowing something *through personal experience*. When they spoke of knowing God, they always used the term that conveys an intimate, personal, experiential relationship. The intensity of the term is found in the King James Version translation of Genesis 4:1, which speaks of Adam "knowing" his wife in a way that produced a child.

Knowing God is a lifestyle of passionate pursuit—a pursuit of God that leads to an ever-deepening experiential relationship with Him. The goal is not merely to know more *about* God, but to actually know *Him*—intimately and experientially.

BIG THOUGHT:

Knowing God is experiencing a deeper relationship with Him.

How to Know God

We will discuss what it means to "know God" later in our journey (Days 6 and 7). For now, the words of bestselling author and theologian J. I. Packer give us a succinct and helpful guide for starting our journey:

> How can we turn our knowledge about God into knowledge of God? The rule for doing this is simple but demanding. It is that we turn each truth that we learn about God into matter for meditation before God, leading to prayer and praise to God.[1]

Quote to Ponder

> The highest science, the loftiest speculation, the mightiest philosophy, which can ever engage the attention of a child of God, is the name, the nature, the person, the work, the doings, and the existence of the great God whom he calls his Father.
> C. H. SPURGEON[2]

Questions to Consider

1. What are some of the biblical reasons given for knowing God? Which one(s) resonated most deeply with you? Why?
2. According to this chapter, what is the difference between knowing God and knowing *about* God?

CORRECTING FALSE VIEWS OF GOD

More Than "The Man Upstairs"

When I was a student in high school, I worked evenings and week-ends at a restaurant. The cook on my shift was a rough, wild-eyed, Vietnam veteran named Ben. He was a very broken, bat-tered man who could be biting in his sarcasm and cynicism. But I liked him.

One night, sitting with Ben in the breakroom, we talked about God. Ben looked at me and said, "Kid, I have my own views of God. In my way of thinking, the Man Upstairs is pretty busy trying to run the universe up there. He doesn't have much inter-est in what is going on in my miserable life down here."

A mixture of anger and pity churned inside me. I was too afraid to say it, but I wanted to shout, "The God of the Bible is more than 'The Man Upstairs.' He is so much better! Your life will continue to be messed up until you figure that out."

In this book, I want to help you get to know the true God of the Bible, the One who is so much more than The Man Upstairs. As we begin to study Him, let's look at several common views about God and compare them to the truth.

The Man Upstairs

My friend Ben's view of God was that He is merely a slightly larger version of us. Ben viewed God as distant and distracted, as very busy and overwhelmed by earth's many problems. God was frus-trated and grumpy—the universe is old and breaking down, and it's all He can do to keep it running. God is either not interested in our problems or has no time to help us through them.

Years ago, I saw a Christian comedian act out this viewpoint. He played God as a rumpled, middle-aged man with a few days of stubble on his face. He was wearing a ball cap and smoking a cigar. He sat at a disheveled desk surrounded by phones that kept ringing.

St. Peter, the angel Gabriel, and people all over the world were calling God about problems, but He could not keep up. When people showed up at God's office with prayer requests, He told them to go away because He was too busy.

This is how many people view God. But He is so much more than just The Man Upstairs.

GOD IS NOT A MAN

"God is not a man. . . . Has he ever spoken and failed to act? Has he ever promised and not carried it through?" (Numbers 23:19 NLT). Anytime we try to picture God as a mere man we do Him and ourselves a great disservice. Even though God often used human images to describe Himself (as a father, a shepherd, or a king), He is much more than any one image can convey. God is so much more than any man.

GOD IS AN INFINITE SPIRIT

"God is spirit" (John 4:24). God is a Being wholly beyond man. He is on a completely different dimension. He is an invisible, infinite spirit.

We humans are limited to our bodies and by our bodies. We can only be in one place at a time. God though, is not bound by a body. He is so much more than a body. He is the divine, infinite Spirit.

GOD IS UNLIMITED

He is infinite. And this shows itself in three amazing ways.

First, *God is omnipresent*. He is not bound by space. "Great is the LORD and most worthy of praise; his greatness no one can fathom" (Psalm 145:3). "Behold, heaven and the heaven of heavens cannot contain You" (1 Kings 8:27 NKJV). God has never said,

"I can only be in one place at a time"—He can be anywhere and everywhere He wants to be, at exactly the same time. He can be here *and* down the street *and* across town *and* in Australia *and* on the moon, all at once. God is not a man.

Second, *God is omnipotent*. That means He is unlimited in terms of strength. Jeremiah declared, "Nothing is too hard for you" (Jeremiah 32:17). God has infinite amounts of strength, energy, and power. He never has been or ever will be busy, tired, overwhelmed, or stressed out. He has never said, "Oh, that's just too hard for Me." He is not wringing His hands in heaven because the details of the universe are more than He can handle.

Third, *God is omniscient*. He has an unlimited mental capacity. If every one of the billions of people on earth prayed to Him at the same moment, none would get a busy signal. God can handle billions with the same intimacy as He can handle one (see Matthew 10:30).

God is not man. He is infinitely beyond any human—*He is God*. He is much more than "The Man Upstairs." And He is also much more than an out-of-touch-old man.

An Out-of-Touch Old Man

A variation of the Man Upstairs is the view that God is a worn-out, old-fashioned, out-of-touch old man. When some people think of God, they see a weary old guy with a long, white beard. Maybe He's wearing a bathrobe, sitting in a rocking chair, doing a crossword puzzle. Next to Him is an end table covered with pill bottles and old newspapers. Most of the time, the old man is asleep.

If you tried to engage this old man in conversation, you'd find that His memory is bad. Oh, He does remember the good old days, when He created the universe and parted the Red Sea. But His ability to do miracles passed a very long time ago. Now, He's retired. He has no strength, no insight, and no ability to help with the difficult and complex problems you are facing today. The world has passed Him by.

Unfortunately, this is how many of us view God. But God is so much more than an out-of-touch old man. He is eternal and changeless.

GOD HAS EXISTED FOREVER

When speaking to God, the psalm writer David said, "My days are like the evening shadow; I wither away like grass. But you, O LORD, sit enthroned forever; your renown endures through all generations" (Psalm 102:11–12).

God is eternal. God always was and always will be. There was not a moment when He came *into* being, because He has always been and perpetually *is* being. There will never be a moment when He ceases to be.

Along these lines, we also recognize that *God is infinite.* He dwells outside the realm of space and time, and He is the only person or thing in the universe that can make that claim. (We'll discuss God's eternal and infinite nature in greater detail on Days 15 and 16.)

GOD HAS NOT CHANGED

PSALM 102:25–27 tells us,

> In the beginning you [God] laid the foundations of the earth, and the heavens are the work of your hands. They will perish, but you remain; they will all wear out like a garment. Like clothing you will change them and they will be discarded. But you remain the same, and your years will never end.

God is infinitely perfect. As such, He has no need ever to change.

Because He is infinite and outside the realm of space and time, God is not one day older today than He was yesterday, or last week, or last month, or last millennium. He never becomes weaker or tired. He is not out-of-date or behind the times:

> Every good gift and every perfect gift is from above, and comes down from the Father of lights, with whom there is no variation or shadow of turning.
> JAMES 1:17 NKJV

> Jesus Christ is the same yesterday and today and forever.
> HEBREWS 13:8

God is eternal. He dwells in a never-ending present. He understands modern technology, and He has understood it for the last ten thousand years. God is not an out-of-touch old-timer. He is as relevant today as He ever was or will be. We change, but God is changeless.

God is active

And we know that in all things God works for the good of those who love him, who have been called according to his purpose.
Romans 8:28

God did not retire at the end of the first century or after World War II. He is as active today as He ever has been. The problem is not the activity level of God, but whether or not we as humans cooperate with His working. The issue is this: Are we where God is working, or are we off doing our own thing?

God is not an old, retired man. He is working. He is still on the job. He is still the Almighty God.

BIG THOUGHT:

God is much more than any man. He is GOD!

Quote to Consider

Many men and women today are living, often with inner dissatisfaction, without any faith in God at all. This is not because they are particularly wicked or selfish or, as the old-fashioned would say, "godless," but because they have not found with their adult minds a God big enough to "account for" life, big enough to "fit in with" the new scientific age, big enough to command their highest admiration and respect, and consequently their willing co-operation.
J. B. Phillips [1]

Questions to Ponder

1. Would you say that your view of God is more that of "The Man Upstairs" or the "Out-of-Touch Old-Timer" or something else?

2. Which of the verses quoted in this chapter caught your attention? Why?

CORRECTING FALSE VIEWS OF GOD

Not a Distant Dad or Genie in a Lamp

What was your father like?

My dad was a very good man. He was honest, generous, God-fearing, intelligent, and very hardworking.

But, like many dads in his generation, he was also distracted and emotionally distant.

My earthly father was a small business owner. He went to the office early in the morning and got home at six o'clock in the evening. He usually spent the rest of the evening reading. But even when he was home, he often was "not home." His mind was on his business.

I came along when my dad was older, and in some ways he was "done parenting." He could not remember my birth date. When asked, he did not know for sure what grade I was in. At one point, he spent more than a month calling me by my older brother's first name. My dad didn't tell me that he loved me until I was in my twenties—and then only after I tricked him into saying it.

My older brother had found that a way to attract Dad's attention was by getting in trouble. I tried to win his attention by getting my name in the newspaper, either for making the dean's list or for accomplishing something in sports.

Fortunately, in the last several years of his life, Dad changed. He and I became close. We ate lunch together weekly and he became in many ways my best friend.

A Distracted Dad?

One challenge of my life has been that my default view of God is that of my earthly father—distant and distracted. In the back of my mind, I think, *God is a very good person, but I should not expect to have a very close relationship with him.*

But when the Bible describes God as our heavenly Father, it paints a much different picture. We find that God is a loving and attentive Father.

Maybe your earthly father was a great dad. Maybe he was not. Realize that the heavenly Father *is* a great father. He is wise, strong, good, loving—and interested in you.

GOD, THE FATHER, LOVES YOU

> *See what great love the Father has lavished on us, that we should be called children of God!*
> 1 JOHN 3:1

This incredible statement is a concise translation of a Greek statement that is even more expansive. I render it as,

> *"Wow! Out of this world! Unbelievable, indescribable, undeniable is the awesome, wonderful, amazingly tremendous love God has poured all over us and out to us and into us. He has even called us—us, the rebellious, self-centered, whiny us—as His very own children!"*

GOD, THE FATHER, KNOWS YOU

Each human has an average of 100,000 hair follicles on his or her head. (These days, I have considerably fewer.) The God who knows everything, knows everything about you—including how many hairs are on your head.

> *"Are not five sparrows sold for two copper coins? And not one of them is forgotten before God. But the very hairs of your head are all numbered. Do not fear therefore; you are of more value than many sparrows."*
> LUKE 12:6–7 NKJV

Think about it: God knows if you have 100,087 hairs or if you have 99,068.

He knows every detail of your life.

Your heavenly Father knows what you ate for breakfast today, or if you ate breakfast. He knows what you did last night. He knows what you are thinking right now.

GOD, THE FATHER, CARES ABOUT YOU

As a father has compassion on his children, so the LORD has compassion on those who fear him.
PSALM 103:13

Maybe you feel as though no one loves you or cares about you. But that is not true. *You need to know that God does.* He is not too busy to be bothered with your problems. He is not too tired to listen. He is not preoccupied. He is not a distracted dad. God is lovingly attentive because He cares about us.

GOD, THE FATHER, IS NEAR HIS HURTING CHILDREN

Someone asked a father of eight children which one he loved best. He said that he loved them all, but he felt closest to whichever one needed him most at that time.

Maybe you are brokenhearted today. Maybe you are crushed in spirit. God is near. His arms are open to you. He loves you. He cares about you. He is attentive to your cries for help.

The LORD is close to the brokenhearted and saves those who are crushed in spirit.
PSALM 34:18

God is not a distracted dad.

He also is not a mere "genie in a lamp."

Genie God

Many people have the idea that God is like a genie. They view God as if He were a supernatural creature trapped in a lamp. When He is released, He has the power to grant us our wishes.

"The Genie God" is powerful, but not invincible. He does

have some expectations of us, a code of conduct that He'd like us to abide by (for example, the Ten Commandments).

When we view God as a genie, we believe we can release Him from His lamp when we need Him—like when we, or someone close to us, goes into the hospital or has some other serious problem. But we also have the power to put God back into the lamp when we are finished with Him.

When God is out of His lamp, He can grant our wishes and bring us good luck. So we take Him out on special occasions like Christmas and Easter, weddings and funerals. We take a few minutes to feel sentimental about Him. But we always stuff Him back in His lamp afterward.

For many of us, God occupies a larger lamp, called "church," on Sundays. In church people sing songs about how strong and kind the Genie God is. But at noon, when the worship service ends, He is usually sent back into His lamp again. During the week, we might get God out of the lamp to help our team in the big game—afterward, one of the players may even acknowledge that he was helped by the Genie God. But regardless of the outcome of the game, God is returned to the lamp and quickly forgotten.

Only fanatics risk letting the Genie stay out of His lamp when they're anywhere other than church. Only a few ever take Him to work or school. Practically no one lets Him out of the lamp on Friday nights.

We like this view of God because it allows us to control Him, to use Him for our purposes. At least that's what we want to believe. The truth is that God is much more than a genie.

GOD IS TOO BIG FOR ANY LAMP

You cannot put God in a lamp. The true God does not fit in anybody's lamp. He is too big and too mighty to be forced into confinement.

> *"But will God really dwell on earth? The heavens,*
> *even the highest heaven, cannot contain you.*
> *How much less this temple I have built!"*
> 1 KINGS 8:27

*"Who can hide in secret places so that I cannot
see them?" declares the LORD. "Do not I fill
heaven and earth?" declares the LORD.*
JEREMIAH 23:24

GOD IS TOO MIGHTY TO FIT INTO YOUR LAMP

The true God is not in anybody's lamp. He is almighty. He can do more than we can even imagine. God is not some silly genie who pops out when you rub the lamp in just the right way. The only lamp God is in is some lamp in our minds.

> *"Ah, Sovereign LORD, you have made the heavens and
> the earth by your great power and outstretched
> arm. Nothing is too hard for you."*
> JEREMIAH 32:17

> *Now to him who is able to do immeasurably more
> than all we ask or imagine, according to his
> power that is at work within us. . .*
> EPHESIANS 3:20

For years I tried to keep God in that "Sunday morning and emergency lamp." It seemed to me that's the way most everyone at my church did it.

But I was miserable. I knew it was wrong, yet I was afraid to let God out of the lamp. Once He was out, I knew I could not control Him.

I decided just to keep God in a lamp all the time and to do my life my way. I still went to church, but I kept God in a lamp by ignoring Him.

Then I really became miserable.

Finally, one day I became tired of playing that game. "God in a lamp" was not real, and my life was not working. Fortunately, the true God was *not* in my lamp, and I realized He had been pursuing me all along. I got down on my knees and told Him,

"I surrender. Instead of trying to use and control You, I surrender myself. You can use and control me as You want. I let You out of the lamp and into my life. I let You into every part of my life. I let You into every day of my week. I will allow You to be God in my life."

What a difference it *made*.
What a difference it *makes*.
What a difference it *can make for you*.

BIG THOUGHT:

God is a loving Father.
He is too big to be controlled.
We need to submit to His control.

Quote to Ponder

Believers do not come to God in prayer as mere subjects to a king in his court. They crawl into the lap of a heavenly Father as a child who comes for protection or help.
ELMER TOWNS[1]

Questions to Consider

1. Which of these two false views of God would apply most to your thinking?
2. In this chapter, what was said about God that you found especially challenging?

CORRECTING FALSE VIEWS OF GOD

Much Better Than an Impersonal Force

I admit that I am a fan of *Star Wars*, at least of the original trilogy of George Lucas films—*Star Wars* (1977), *The Empire Strikes Back* (1980), and *Return of the Jedi* (1983). Like many others, I am a sucker for the good-versus-evil plotline, the story of the selfless Rebel Alliance fighting to free the galaxy from the clutches of the oppressive Empire. I also like the journey Luke Skywalker takes to become a Jedi knight.

However, I am not a fan of the films' theological aspects. The series promotes a mystical power known as "the Force," which is described by the great Jedi Obi-wan Kenobi as "an energy field created by all living things [that] surrounds us, penetrates us, [and] binds the galaxy together."[1] The lucky ones who are genetically tied most deeply to the Force have special abilities, and through special training, they can achieve supernatural feats such as telekinesis, clairvoyance, precognition, and mind-control. The Jedi are those who harness the light side of the Force; the Sith manipulate its dark side through anger and aggression.

An Impersonal Force

Unfortunately, many people have adopted such nonsense as their predominant theology. They have a vague, pantheistic, impersonal view of God.

Many have also adopted the Hindu and Buddhist concept of karma. That basically means that good thoughts and actions in this life yield good results in the future, while bad behaviors lead to trouble and suffering. Karma is all about cause and effect—

it's an impartial, impersonal energy something like the Force of *Star Wars*.

However, while the God of the Bible is the driving Force behind everything, He is much more than an impersonal energy field. He is the greatest Person in the universe.

God Is a Person

God is not a thing but a person. That is not to say He is a human being, but He possesses "personality." God created humans in His own image. He has rational consciousness of His own being. He has personal names. He has intellect, emotions, and will. Let's consider several of these points in greater detail.

GOD HAS PERSONAL NAMES

Jesus referred to God as His Father (Matthew 11:25) and told us to address God as "our Father" (Matthew 6:9). God's children are invited to call Him "Abba," which is like saying, "Daddy" (Galatians 4:6).

GOD HAS PERSONAL CHARACTERISTICS

For example, He is said to have the capacity to love. God declared, "Yes, I have loved you with an everlasting love; therefore with lovingkindness I have drawn you" (Jeremiah 31:3 NKJV). He "so loved the world" that He sent His Son, Jesus, to die as punishment for human sin (John 3:16). Jesus' death on the cross was how God "demonstrates his own love for us" (Romans 5:8).

GOD IS DESCRIBED AS HAVING PERSONAL FEELINGS

A psalm writer told us that God "loves righteousness and justice" (Psalm 33:5). God is said to have been "sorry" that He made humankind on the earth and "was grieved in His heart" (Genesis 6:6 NKJV). Jesus stood weeping outside the tomb of His friend Lazarus (John 11:35). James reminded us that "the Lord is full of compassion and mercy" (James 5:11).

God can get angry. Once He told Moses, "Let Me alone, that My wrath may burn hot against [the Israelites] and I may consume them" (Exodus 32:10 NKJV). He laughs (Psalm 2:4), though that is derisive laughter over the opposition of puny humans. But one day, God will respond to His own people with a great display of joy: "He will rejoice over you with gladness, He will quiet you with His love, He will rejoice over you with singing" (Zephaniah 3:17 NKJV).

The Lord Possesses a Will to Act as He Pleases

Paul declared that he was called to be an apostle by the will of God (1 Corinthians 1:1). The psalmist wrote, "Our God is in heaven; He does whatever He pleases" (Psalm 115:3 NKJV). Isaiah recorded the Lord's declaration, "Everything I plan will come to pass, for I do whatever I wish" (Isaiah 46:10 NLT).

God Can Change His Mind

Jonah spoke of the Lord relenting of His commitment to destroy the wicked people of Nineveh: "When God saw what they had done and how they had put a stop to their evil ways, he changed his mind and did not carry out the destruction he had threatened" (Jonah 3:10 NLT).

God Has the Intellectual Ability to Create Plans for His People

In one of the Bible's most encouraging promises, God declares, "For I know the plans I have for you. . .plans for good and not for disaster, to give you a future and a hope" (Jeremiah 29:11 NLT).

God is not merely an impersonal, unfeeling force. He is the very personal God.

God Is Alive

The apostle Paul lauded Christians in Thessalonica for their dramatic and exemplary conversion, as the Word of God was thundering out from them. Their amazing transformation did not occur by believing in an impersonal force or a dead idol. Rather, it was the result of embracing the living God:

> You became followers of us and of the Lord, having received the word in much affliction, with joy of the Holy Spirit, so that you became examples to all in Macedonia and Achaia who

*believe. For from you the word of the Lord has sounded forth,
not only in Macedonia and Achaia, but also in every place.
Your faith toward God has gone out, so that we do not need to
say anything. For they themselves declare concerning us what
manner of entry we had to you, and how you turned to God
from idols to serve the living and true God.*
1 THESSALONIANS 1:6–9 NKJV

Paul's missionary journey took him from Israel to what is modern-day Turkey. In the city of Lystra, he healed a man who had been crippled from birth, and the people went crazy. So Paul took the opportunity to encourage them to abandon their dead idols to serve the living God:

*"We also are men with the same nature as you, and preach
to you that you should turn from these useless things
to the living God, who made the heaven, the earth,
the sea, and all things that are in them."*
ACTS 14:15 NKJV

Paul was likely familiar with the words of a psalmist, who had written centuries earlier,

*Whatever the LORD pleases He does, in heaven and in earth,
in the seas and in all deep places. . . . The idols of the
nations are silver and gold, the work of men's hands.
They have mouths, but they do not speak; eyes they
have, but they do not see; they have ears, but they
do not hear, nor is there any breath in their mouths.*
PSALM 135:6, 15–17 NKJV

God Is the Greatest Force in the Universe

God is more than an impersonal force, but He is also more than merely a living person. He is the greatest force in the universe. Jeremiah, Jesus, and Isaiah make this abundantly clear.

"Ah, Lord GOD! Behold, You have made the heavens and the

earth by Your great power and outstretched arm.
There is nothing too hard for You."
JEREMIAH 32:17 NKJV

"With men this is impossible, but with God
all things are possible."
MATTHEW 19:26 NKJV

The LORD of hosts has sworn saying, "Surely, just as I have
intended so it has happened, and just as I have planned
so it will stand. . . . For the LORD of hosts has planned,
and who can frustrate it? And as for His stretched-out
hand, who can turn it back?"
ISAIAH 14:24, 27 NASB

God Is the Greatest Person in the Universe

The Bible repeatedly declares the greatness of God. For example:

No one is like you, LORD; you are great,
and your name is mighty in power.
JEREMIAH 10:6

Great is the LORD and most worthy of praise;
he is to be feared above all gods.
PSALM 96:4

Yours, LORD, is the greatness and the power and the glory and
the majesty and the splendor, for everything in heaven and
earth is yours. Yours, LORD, is the kingdom; you are exalted as
head over all.
1 CHRONICLES 29:11

God is just some impersonal force? Don't believe that for a
second.

BIG THOUGHT:

God is the greatest, most powerful, living person.

Quote

> *Comfort and peace can never come from anything we know about ourselves, but only and always from what we know about Him. . . . Nothing can set our hearts at rest but a real acquaintance with God.*
> HANNAH WHITALL SMITH[2]

Questions to Consider

1. Which of the following characteristics of God do you find most comforting: that He is alive, that He is a person, or that He is supremely powerful? Why?
2. Have you found the quoted words of Hannah Whitall Smith to be true in your life? When?

DAY

5

CORRECTING FALSE VIEWS OF GOD

Not a Cosmic Killjoy

When I was sixteen, I had a very immature view of life and God. I struggled to truly trust that God's plans involved my best interests, and I was afraid if I totally surrendered my life to Him, He would make me miserable. I thought of God as a cosmic killjoy.

My thinking went something like this (remember, I was only sixteen): I liked living in the United States. The only other country I even wanted to visit was England. Being afraid of snakes, I never wanted to visit Africa. Somehow, I figured God would make me go there, and I would run into snakes. . .or cannibals.

I loved riding my bicycle. My friend Scott and I had once ridden 954 miles from southern Ohio to Montreal, Canada, in ten days. I feared that God would take that kind of experience away from me.

Since I'm relatively short, I was too insecure to date girls who were more than an inch or two taller than I was. I was afraid that if I gave every aspect of my life to God, He would make me marry a very tall (and probably mean and homely) woman. To make matters worse, I was sure that He would then send us to Africa as missionaries to cannibals, in an area infested with huge snakes.

I was reluctant to believe that God was really good—that His will would be best. But eventually, I tired of running from God and His will. My life was going nowhere. I was empty, lonely, and depressed.

Finally, I got down on my knees and surrendered. I told God, "I don't know why You would want my life, but as of right now,

I give all I know of myself to all I know of You. Whatever that means, be the Lord of my life."

On a blank piece of paper I wrote "God's Will for My Life" across the top. I left the rest of the page blank. Then I signed and dated the bottom, like a contract, so God could fill in whatever *He* wished—even if that meant Africa and snakes.

In His great kindness, one of the first things the Lord wrote on that "contract" was "The England Bicycle Evangelistic Team." That summer, I spent seven weeks in England and two in Scotland riding a bike and doing evangelism!

Then I met Cathy, the woman I married. She is pretty, petite, and very sweet.

A few years ago, my youngest son and I visited Africa as missionaries. We loved it. And we did not see a single snake or cannibal.

Certainly, over the years, God has written some very challenging things on my contract. But even though His long-term purposes took precedence over my short-term pleasure, I can look back and see that what was hard at the time ended up bringing good into my life and the lives of others.

I know from experience that God is not a cosmic killjoy.

Cosmic Killjoy

The notion that God is a cosmic killjoy goes all the way back to the Garden of Eden, where Lucifer tempted Eve, the very first woman. Notice his opening line:

> *Now the serpent was more crafty than any of the wild animals the LORD God had made. He said to the woman, "Did God really say, 'You must not eat from any tree in the garden'?"*
> GENESIS 3:1

Satan's first recorded words to a human being were an attempt to paint God as a cosmic killjoy. But Eve stood her ground—for a while.

> *The woman said to the serpent, "We may eat fruit from the trees in the garden, but God did say, 'You must not eat fruit*

from the tree that is in the middle of the garden, and you must not touch it, or you will die.'"
GENESIS 3:2–3

So, Lucifer shifted his approach slightly. First, he implied that God is not truthful. Then he told Eve that God is mean to withhold from her the potential of divine illumination.

"You will not certainly die," the serpent said to the woman. "For God knows that when you eat from it your eyes will be opened, and you will be like God, knowing good and evil."
GENESIS 3:4–5

You know the rest of the story. Satan's words were enough to persuade Eve to eat the forbidden fruit and give some to Adam—thus plunging the world under the curse of sin.

Make no mistake, "cosmic killjoy" is a dangerous misrepresentation of God.

The Truth: God Is Good

The psalms are full of statements about the goodness of God. The true God *is* good and *does* good. His will and ways are good.

You are good, and do good.
PSALM 119:68 NKJV

Oh, give thanks to the LORD, for He is good! For His mercy endures forever.
PSALM 107:1 NKJV

The LORD is good to all, and His tender mercies are over all His works.
PSALM 145:9 NKJV

Oh, how great is Your goodness, which You have laid up for those who fear You, which You have prepared for those who trust in You.
PSALM 31:19 NKJV

Oh, taste and see that the Lord is good;
blessed is the man who trusts in Him!
Psalm 34:8 NKJV

God's Will for Us Is Good

Dear brothers and sisters, I plead with you to give your bodies
to God because of all he has done for you. Let them be a living
and holy sacrifice—the kind he will find acceptable. This is truly
the way to worship him. Don't copy the behavior and customs
of this world, but let God transform you into a new person by
changing the way you think. Then you will learn to know God's
will for you, which is good and pleasing and perfect.
Romans 12:1–2 NLT

Notice the first sentence, in which Paul calls us to give our entire selves to God. Then notice that the last sentence, in which he told us that God's will is good, pleasing, and perfect. It only makes sense that a good God would have good desires toward us—and a good plan for us.

Paul had written earlier that "in all things God works for the good of those who love him, who have been called according to his purpose" (Romans 8:28). God's plan for every event in your life is for ultimate good.

Of course, that doesn't mean that everything we experience is good or pleasant or fun in itself. That does mean that God will use even the hard, difficult, painful events of our lives to bring about good. Usually the good is our growth in godliness (Romans 8:29, James 1:2–4). Often our hard times refine our faith (1 Peter 1:6–7). Sometimes our painful seasons enable us to better minister to others as they suffer (2 Corinthians 1:3–4). No doubt bad things will happen to us for which we may not see good results until we get to glory. But make no mistake: God works every event in our lives for ultimate good.

The psalm writer David was herding sheep when God chose him to be Israel's second (and greatest) king. He wrote that when the Lord is *our* shepherd, all sorts of good things happen—we are given direction, provision, restoration, affirmation, correction, and protection (Psalm 23:1–5). In fact, "goodness and love will follow" us throughout our lives (Psalm 23:6).

In another section of scripture, we read of the goodness of God's plans for His people. After seventy years of punishment for the Old Testament Israelites' disobedience and idolatry, God planned to return them to their land and bless them:

> *"For I know the plans I have for you," declares the*
> *LORD, "plans to prosper you and not to harm*
> *you, plans to give you hope and a future."*
> JEREMIAH 29:11

God promises that His plans for His people give hope. They are not for our pain, but for our good and prosperity.

God's Presence Is a Place of Life, Joy, and Pleasure

> *You will show me the path of life; in Your presence is fullness*
> *of joy; at Your right hand are pleasures forevermore.*
> PSALM 16:11 NKJV

Those in the presence of God are not suffering pain at the hands of a cosmic killjoy. They are experiencing life, joy, and pleasure because they are near the true God. The reason heaven will be such a good experience is because of the radiant goodness of God's very nature.

God Looks at His Children with Joy, Not Meanness or Anger

There is a sweet promise of a coming day that tells us much about the good nature of God:

> *In that day it will be said to Jerusalem: "Do not be afraid,*
> *O Zion; Do not let your hands fall limp. The LORD your God*
> *is in your midst, a Warrior who saves. He will rejoice over you*
> *with joy; He will be quiet in His love [making no mention of*
> *your past sins], He will rejoice over you with shouts of joy."*
> ZEPHANIAH 3:16–17 AMP

That doesn't sound like a cosmic killjoy to me.

BIG THOUGHT:

God is good and views His children with joy.

Quotes to Consider

He [Jesus] concealed something. . . . There was something that He hid from all men. . .some one thing that was too great for God to show us when He walked our earth; and I have sometimes fancied that it was His mirth [joy].
G. K. CHESTERTON[1]

What could very well be the most obvious, most overlooked, most disregarded, most neglected, most misunderstood, most undefined, most manipulated left-behind, swept-under-the-carpet-and-barred-from-hallowed-church-halls reality in all of Christendom: that Jesus was a man of joy.
BRUCE MARCHIANO[2]

Questions to Ponder

1. Which of the Bible verses mentioned in this chapter jumped out at you? Why?
2. In what area of your life do you struggle to trust that God has your best interests in mind?

HOW TO KNOW GOD

Knowing God through Stillness, Silence, Solitude, and Seeking Him

I wasn't really a bad kid, but I was always an active child. I spent a great amount of time during my early elementary years in the corner or visiting the principal simply because I could not keep still.

I vividly remember one evening when my mom came home from an open house at my school. The first thing she asked was, "Dave, why didn't you tell me where your desk was?"

"I did," I replied. "I told you that it was next to the teacher's."

She shook her head and sighed, "Yes, but when you said 'next to the teacher's,' I thought you meant the front row. I did not think you meant right up *next to* the teacher's."

In first grade, the girl who sat behind me was named Patricia. She was one of those always perfect, always clean, always quiet, straight-A, teacher's pet kind of kids. You know the type. Maybe some of you were that type.

I wasn't.

Easily bored, I was always saying, "Hey, Patricia, look at that. Hey, Patricia, watch this."

Probably a dozen times every day she would lean forward and say, "Keep still, Dave Earley. You won't learn anything. Keep still." I can still hear her voice telling me, "Keep still."

My best day of first grade was the only time Patricia ever got in trouble. She got in trouble because, of all things, she was talking.

She was telling *someone* to "keep still."

Now, there are times I hear God say, "Dave, keep still. You won't learn anything. Quiet your soul. Slow down. Get off the fast lane. Jump off the treadmill. Stop doing. Start being. Be still."

Does God ever say to you, *"Be still. I can't do anything with you because your world is too busy, too cluttered, too crowded, and too loud"*? I imagine He might say to you, as He has to me, *"You are busy about many things, and you are neglecting the one thing that is most needed. Your world is too loud to hear my voice. It is too cluttered to see my hand. It is too crowded to feel my touch."*[1]

"Know That I Am God"

> *"Be still, and know that I am God."*
> PSALM 46:10

The words *be still* literally mean "stop!" They speak of ceasing activity and coming to a point of absolute rest.

The word *know* used by the psalmist can be understood as "intimately experience." In other words, this verse could be rendered, "Be still and intimately experience God." When our hearts are not still, we won't easily experience Him.

God speaks through a still, small voice. When I am not still, I struggle to sense God. Without the intentional practice of stillness, silence, and solitude, I fail to experience God as much as I desire, or get as much of God as I would hope.

"Hear My Voice"

> *"My sheep hear My voice, and I know them,*
> *and they follow Me."*
> JOHN 10:27 NKJV

As above, the word *know* here also speaks of "intimate, personal experience." Jesus wanted His sheep to know Him in an intimate, ongoing, personal, experiential, and relational way.

The tense of the verb *hear* indicates that Jesus' sheep hear His voice more than once. His sheep are literally to "continue to hear" His voice so they can "continue to follow" Him.

As Rod Dempsey and I wrote in our book *Spiritual Formation Is*,

> We can't hear His voice if we are doing all the talking. Therefore, listening in stillness and expectant silence is an essential discipline for us to develop. There are times when the Lord says, "Be quiet. Stop talking. Stop analyzing. Just listen. You are not ready to follow My voice until you are quiet enough to hear My voice."[2]

"Taste and See That the Lord Is Good"

I have a confession to make: *I am addicted to the psalms.* I read them almost daily, and I particularly enjoy those written by David—especially the ones he composed in the wilderness while running from Saul. One of these "Fugitive Psalms" that I especially like is Psalm 34. David wrote it after pretending to be crazy to escape the Philistines. (Craziness is something to which I can relate.)

In such an awful circumstance, I'd expect David to complain about the rank injustice of his situation or about his extreme misfortune—but he did not. Instead he resolved to praise the Lord. As he did, David mused on the blessings he'd received from God, and then made an amazing observation:

> Oh, taste and see that the LORD is good;
> blessed is the man who trusts in Him!
> PSALM 34:8 NKJV

This is true spirituality. David had developed a personal knowledge of God that was so real and sweet that he declared the goodness of God in the worst of times. He knew that God was trustworthy no matter what.

"Wait on the Lord"

The spiritually strong are those who wait on the Lord.

> Even the youths shall faint and be weary, and the young men shall utterly fall, but those who wait on the LORD shall renew

their strength; they shall mount up with wings like eagles, they
shall run and not be weary, they shall walk and not faint.
Isaiah 40:30–31 NKJV

"Waiting on the Lord" is an essential secret of spiritual freshness, fullness, centeredness, and strength. The concept of waiting involves time and speaks of place. When we "wait on" someone, we set aside time for them. In Isaiah 40, "waiting" further speaks of active reliance and determined trust.

A Spiritual Retreat

Maybe you are like me: I tend to live an overcommitted life that has no margins. I don't crowd my life with bad things, but I jam it so full of good things that there is little room for the best things. Then life itself steadily bombards me with troubles and trials. Quickly I find my soul swimming with worries, fears, and frustrations. It all crowds out God, drowns out His voice, and leaves me drained and empty.

At one point, I desperately needed to break the cycle of work addiction and burnout. I needed to hear God's voice about the future. I was spiritually empty, emotionally drained, and physically battling illness. I seriously needed to know God in the manner we are discussing in this chapter.

Sensing this need for space in my soul, I scheduled a spiritual retreat where I could spend forty-eight hours in the disciplines of silence, stillness, solitude, journaling, and prayer. I got out of town and alone with God. No phone, no internet, no TV, no music. It was just my Bible, my notebook, me, and God.

At first, it was very uncomfortable. I struggled to be truly still. My mind spun with thoughts and ideas and "stuff I need to do." I paced. It was hard just to be quiet before God.

So, I sat down and took a few deep breaths. Then I pulled out my journal and slowly and silently began to work through several types of prayer: Adoration, Confession, Thanksgiving, and Surrender, as well as Forgiving people who'd hurt me.

As my stillness level increased, the Holy Spirit began to unload my crowded heart. It felt awkward, yet good, to sense

Him carrying burdens out of my soul—and lifting weight off my shoulders.

Initially, I was uneasy, because I wasn't "making something happen." But what I failed to realize was that something significant *was* happening.

I discussed this in *Spiritual Formation Is*:

As my heart became less crowded, God became more real. His presence tenderly, quietly, peacefully began to flow into the newly vacated areas of my soul. I began to discern God's heartbeat slowly, deeply, firmly, pounding out love and hope with each beat. His still small voice gave me encouragement and a plan for the next chapter in my life. As I experienced a great calming in my soul, I realized just how tense, stressed, anxious, busy, cluttered, and empty I had let myself become in the previous months.

The best part of my forty-eight hours of silence and stillness was not the forty-eight hours themselves, although they were wonderful. The best part was the space created during those forty-eight hours. As a result, I had more room for God. For months afterward I felt, heard, and tasted God more often, more deeply, and more clearly than before.[3]

Most of us aren't able to schedule forty-eight-hour retreats very often, but we can be intentional about building into our daily schedules silence, stillness, solitude, and seeking God.

BIG THOUGHT:

God-seekers through the ages have found a special daily connection with God essential. This usually involves three aspects: a time, a place, and a plan.

A *TIME*

Most people meet with God first thing in the morning, but there have been seasons of my life when my time was over lunch or late at night after everyone else had gone to bed.

My time for meeting with God daily is or will be:

A PLACE

I usually meet with God in my study, but there have been seasons when it was in my bed, at the kitchen table, on a walk, or in my car.

My place for meeting with God daily is or will be:

A PLAN

The plan usually involves a mixture of Bible reading and prayer. Many of us also include journaling and some form of worship.

My plan for meeting with God daily is or will be:

Quote to Consider

> *Jesus urged his disciples to take time out. Following Jesus cannot be done at a sprint. If we want to follow someone, we can't go faster than the one who is leading.*
> JOHN ORTBERG [4]

Questions to Ponder

1. Have you ever practiced stillness, silence, solitude, and seeking God as spiritual disciplines?
2. Do you regularly practice stillness, silence, solitude, and seeking God as spiritual disciplines?
3. How do you plan to apply these disciplines to your life this month?
4. When is your daily time, place, and plan for meeting with God?

HOW TO KNOW GOD

Knowing God through Passionate Pursuit

The week before I met Cathy, I came up with what I considered to be a brainstorm. I was a twenty-year-old student at a Christian college with only ten weeks left in the semester. Knowing that I might never again have as good a chance to get to know so many attractive Christian girls, I made a list of the ten I wanted to date. I planned to ask out one girl each week. It would be a delightful dating odyssey.

But then I met Cathy.

That brief encounter ruined my plan, as she jumped to the top spot on my list and became my date the next nine weekends in a row.

I wanted to know all I could about her. I wanted to be with her as much as possible.

But that was more difficult than you might guess. I lived in a dorm on campus, which was located on a mountain outside town. She lived in town, five miles away, with her sister. Neither of us had a car. My dorm housed eighty young men and one telephone. (This was before the proliferation of cell phones, email, and social media.) I wondered how I would ever get to know Cathy better.

But, amazingly, it seemed as though every time I came out of class, she just happened to be nearby, heading to her class. It was weird. I had never noticed her prior to a few weeks earlier, and now she was there all the time. *What an answered prayer*, I thought!

After we were married, I heard Cathy laughing with one of her friends. She was explaining that she had worked for the dean of the school of religion and had used her position to get a copy of *my* class schedule. Because she knew where I'd be, she could "just happen" to be outside my classes when they dismissed.

I was stunned by the realization: *while I thought I was pursuing her, in actuality, she was pursuing me.* Cathy skillfully positioned herself so that I would think I was pursuing her. At first, I was a little angry about the way she'd duped me. But after thinking about it, I became highly grateful that she had gone to all that trouble to get to know me.

As I prayed a few days later, I told God that I was seeking Him with all my heart. Inwardly, I was almost proud of my pursuit. But then it hit me: *Just as Cathy had allowed me to think I was the pursuer when I was actually being pursued by her, God does the same thing.* We think we are discovering God, when—surprisingly—we learn He's been there all along, skillfully positioning Himself just within reach, waiting to be found by us.

God does not hide from us. In fact, He *wants* to be found and for us to know Him. The New Testament writer James said, "Draw near to God and He will draw near to you" (James 4:8 NASB). Twentieth-century pastor A. W. Tozer wrote,

> *We pursue God because, and only because, He has first put an urge within us that spurs us to the pursuit. "No man can come to me," said our Lord, "except the Father which hath sent me draw him" (John 6:44).[1]*

Seek God Out of Desperation

Psalm 63 opens with an interesting superscription: *A psalm of David. When he was in the Desert of Judah.* This reminds us that, like most psalms, the 63rd was forged on the anvil of painful human experience. The beauty of this psalm rises out of the ugly nature of David's experience.

Let me tell you the backstory of this psalm.

When teenage David killed the giant Goliath, he became an instant rock star in Israel. As David continued walking with God, God continued to bless him—and his fame expanded.

King Saul became insanely envious. The Lord was clearly with

David but had left Saul. So the jealous king sent David away to lead a small army of a thousand men. Saul hoped that if David was not killed, he would at least be defeated. But instead of dying or fading into obscurity, David won every battle with the Philistines. After that, his popularity was off the charts (see 1 Samuel 18:28–30).

David's success made King Saul even more psychotic. Saul became intent on killing David. So, for nearly a decade, he and his army hunted David through the Judean wilderness. David had to leave behind his position, his wife, his home, his friends, and his reputation as he ran for his life. David became a fugitive.

Yet, he made a very good choice. The worst brought out David's best. In desperation, he decided to chase after God much more ardently.

> *You, God, are my God, earnestly I seek you; I thirst for you,*
> *my whole being longs for you, in a dry and parched land where*
> *there is no water.*
> PSALM 63:1

The foremost thought on David's mind—and one of the first words out of his mouth—was *God*. David was unashamedly God-centered and God-thirsty. He did not cry out for justice, vengeance, or deliverance. He was not asking for food, drink, or shelter. He yearned for God, thirsted for God, and pined for God.

This was David's secret. This is the passion of those throughout all time who seek and find God—a burning, relentless, undeniable thirst for Him.

When David said that he was earnestly seeking after God, he was saying, *God is so important that I will get up early to go after Him. I wake up with God foremost on my mind. Seeking God is my top priority.*

When he said he thirsted and his whole body longed for God, David meant he was pursuing God with a single-minded devotion that would not stop until it gained what it sought. David spoke of pursuing God with one's entire being, which sounds like the "greatest commandment" that Jesus described: to love the Lord with *all* of your heart, soul, mind, and strength (Matthew 22:37; Deuteronomy 6:5).

Seek God Out of Delight

When David became king, his first official act was to return the ark of the covenant to Jerusalem. He knew that the ark represented God's presence, and he wanted nothing more than for his people to experience that presence for themselves.

As the procession carrying the ark came closer and closer to Jerusalem, David became more and more excited. Eventually, he could not contain himself and he "danced before the LORD with all his might" (2 Samuel 6:14 NKJV).

Later, when his wife confronted him over his "vulgar" behavior, David declared that he would gladly celebrate recklessly, humbly, and in a manner even more undignified than that (2 Samuel 6:21–22). God was His delight.

Even at one of the lowest points of his life, David confidently stated, "Taste and see that the LORD is good" (Psalm 34:8). He encouraged us to "take delight in the LORD, and he will give you the desires of your heart" (Psalm 37:4). He referred to God as "my joy and my delight" (Psalm 43:4).

David sought God because He delighted in God.

Seek God Out of the Discipline of Daily Diligence

We are able to find God in our desperate times and delight in God in the positive times when we have developed a lifestyle of daily diligence. People that know God deeply have developed the discipline to seek Him daily through His Word and in prayer.

David pledged his daily pursuit when he prayed,

> *My voice You shall hear in the morning, O LORD; in the morning I will direct it to You, and I will look up.*
> PSALM 5:3 NKJV

Moses revealed his own God-hungry heart when he pitched a tent outside the camp and went there to speak with the Lord face to face (Exodus 33:7–10). Jeremiah wrote, "'The LORD is my portion,' says my soul, 'Therefore I hope in Him!' The Lord is good to those who wait for Him, to the soul who seeks Him" (Lamentations 3:24–25 NKJV).

Jesus modeled the daily pursuit when, after a long draining day of ministry, He got up early to seek the Lord (Mark 1:35). And the author of Hebrews both warned and promised when he said, "Without faith it is impossible to please Him, for he who comes to God must believe that He is, and that He is a rewarder of those who diligently seek Him" (Hebrews 11:6 NKJV).

The sixteenth century German Reformer Martin Luther once said, "It is a good thing to let prayer be the first business in the morning and the last in the evening."[2] A. W. Tozer wrote, "The man who would know God must give time to Him."[3]

BIG THOUGHT:

God is there. He is waiting to be pursued, so seek Him.

Quote to Ponder

If I could only give one piece of advice to a new Christian, it would be this: Develop the discipline of spending time alone with God every day. . . . There is no substitute for a daily time alone with God.
Billy Graham[4]

Questions to Consider

1. What is your daily time to seek God's face?
2. Where is your daily place to seek God's face?
3. What do you do when you seek God's face?

KNOWING GOD BY HIS NAMES

Elohim, God Strong and Mighty

The summer after my sophomore year in college, a few of us were to represent the school on a seventy-day preaching tour across the United States. My pre-trip assignment was to contact churches and map out the trip from an empty office in the Christian Service Department.

When I walked in the door, there was a beautiful young woman sitting behind the receptionist desk. She had sleek brown hair, sparkling green eyes, and a warm smile.

"Hi," she said with a voice like warm vanilla. "May I help you?"

My heart began to beat wildly while everything else shifted into slow motion. It was as if there was music in the air. My stomach was filled with butterflies. I felt as though I was skiing down a mountainside covered in fresh white snow. This must be love!

Then my eyes shifted to the nameplate on the desk where she sat: MRS. DEB MOQUIN, it read in clear, no-nonsense letters.

Oh no! I thought. *Mrs.? Mrs.? What have I done? How could this happen? I just fell in love with a married woman!*

I averted my eyes, mumbled something about working in the back office, and stumbled past her. Reaching my desk, I put my head in my hands, closed my eyes, took a deep breath, and tried to process what had just happened.

Then Al, the man in charge of the Christian Service Department, burst into my office with a big smile. The beautiful girl from the front desk walked in sheepishly behind him. "Dave, there is someone I want to introduce to you. This is *Miss* Cathy Smith."

I looked puzzled.

"Cathy was sitting at Mrs. Moquin's desk while Mrs. Moquin was on a break."

The girl from the front desk smiled at me.

"Cathy is a freshman, and she is very *single* and available," Al said with a wicked little grin. She glared at him, then smiled at me.

She has been smiling at me ever since.

The Names of God

Getting someone's name and title correct is very important. The more names, titles, and descriptions we have for a person, the better we can understand him or her.

This is especially important with God. As He is infinite, and in every way beyond us, the better we know His names and titles the better we can know Him.

There are three primary names for God in the Old Testament:

- God (*Elohim*)
- Lord (*Jehovah* or *YHWH*)
- Lord (*Adonai*)

Beyond these three, the Old Testament contains more than eighty compound names and titles that use one of these three primary names. In the rest of this chapter, we will look at the first name of God recorded in the Bible: *Elohim*.

Elohim

In the beginning God [Elohim] created
the heavens and the earth.
Genesis 1:1

The first verse in the Bible uses Elohim as the name of God. This verse refutes:

- Atheism: It shows that there *is* a God.
- Agnosticism: It tells us He is knowable by name.
- Polytheism: It tells us that there is only one God.

- Pantheism: It reveals that God created all things, not that God is all things
- Materialism: It shows us that the material world is not god, but rather was made by God.

Elohim is used some thirty times in the first chapter of Genesis and twenty-five hundred times through the rest of the Old Testament. The name *Elohim* is derived from two Hebrew words: *El* meaning "unlimited strength, energy, and power" and *Alah* signifying "to swear, to bind through an oath, to make a covenant." Therefore, *Elohim* speaks of the God who is all-powerful *and* who keeps His promises. Elohim is "the infinitely strong and faithful one."

Grammatically, *Elohim* is a singular noun with a plural ending. This hints at God's tri-unity of Father, Son, and Holy Spirit, a reality we perceive from the whole of the Bible. All three persons of the godhead were involved with creation and are involved in Elohim's ongoing activity.

Elohim Is Strong and Mighty

In the beginning God created the heavens and the earth.
GENESIS 1:1

In Genesis 1, we see that Elohim is *active*, not passive. He "created" (verse 1). He also "saw" (verse 4), "made" (verse 7), and "blessed" (verse 22).

Elohim is supremely creative. He "created the heavens and the earth" (Genesis 1:1). He designed the universe so that no two fingerprints are alike, nor any two snowflakes. The ocean paints a perpetually shifting portrait of blue, green, and gray. Night after night, month after month, year after year, every sunset is unique—and often awe-inspiring. He designed the human body with the ability to grow, develop, even heal itself of many diseases.

Scripture shows us further that Elohim is mighty. He created not only the heavens and the earth, but all that is in them. The apostle John stated, "All things were made through Him, and without Him nothing was made that was made" (John 1:3 NKJV).

Jesus declared the infinite power of God. In discussing the impossibility of saving sinners, Jesus told His disciples, "With man this is impossible, but with God all things are possible" (Matthew 19:26).

David cried out to Elohim, "Summon your might, O God. Display your power, O God, as you have in the past" (Psalm 68:28 NLT). David also pleaded with Israel:

Ascribe strength to God; His excellence is over Israel, and His strength is in the clouds. O God, You are more awesome than Your holy places. The God of Israel is He who gives strength and power to His people. Blessed be God!
PSALM 68:34–35 NKJV

Knowing God as Elohim means recognizing His mighty, creative, active power. When you are weak, you can cry out to Elohim for strength, power, might, and creative activity on your behalf.

Elohim Is Trustworthy
Elohim promised to deliver Noah, his family and the representative animals from the flood, and He did (Genesis 6:17–18; 8:1–2). He promised to perpetually bless, multiply, and protect Abraham and his descendants, to bring them into the Promised land, and to be their Elohim (Genesis 17:1–8). Since then, though it has been a bumpy, occasionally brutal ride for the Jews, Elohim has kept (and will continue to keep) His promise.

Elohim Is Good
In what we know as Psalm 68, David wrote a tribute of sorts to the powerful goodness of Elohim. He encouraged his readers to praise Elohim, then listed several reasons why:

But let the righteous be glad; let them rejoice before God [Elohim]; yes, let them rejoice exceedingly. . . . A father of the fatherless, a defender of widows, is God in His holy habitation. God sets the solitary [lonely] in families;

He brings out those who are bound into prosperity. . . .
You, O God, provided from Your goodness for the poor.
PSALM 68:3, 5–6, 10 NKJV

Notice the five blessings for which Elohim is credited:

- He is a father to orphans.
- He is the champion of widows.
- He places the lonely in families.
- He brings prisoners into freedom and prosperity.
- He provides for the poor.

Elohim Is Strong and Mighty and Trustworthy and Good

Because of the ancient Israelites' rebellion, the first copy of the Ten Commandments had been broken. So, Moses returned to the mountain of God to meet with Him for forty days and nights. Moses came down with the second provision of the Ten Commandments—and gave the people a summary of Elohim's expectations:

> *"And now, Israel, what does the LORD your God [Elohim]*
> *require of you, but to fear the LORD your God, to walk in*
> *all His ways and to love Him, to serve the LORD your God*
> *with all your heart and with all your soul, and to keep*
> *the commandments of the LORD and His statutes*
> *which I command you today for your good?"*
> DEUTERONOMY 10:12–13 NKJV

Moses told the people they should meet these expectations because of Elohim's strength and goodness.

> *"For the LORD your God is God of gods and Lord of lords, the*
> *great God, mighty and awesome, who shows no partiality nor*
> *takes a bribe. He administers justice for the fatherless and the*
> *widow, and loves the stranger, giving him food and clothing."*
> DEUTERONOMY 10:17–18 NKJV

What a combination! Elohim is the strong and mighty God who has a heart for the hurting *and* the power to do something about it *and* the integrity to keep His promises.

To Know Elohim

Moses wanted the Israelites to know and respond to God as Elohim because He alone is almighty and trustworthy. If they did, they would run to Him when they needed help instead of to false gods. David believed that Elohim was worthy of praise. Noah and Abraham found that He could be trusted.

To know God as Elohim is to recognize His creative power *and* good heart. It is to run to Him when you need help. It is to claim His promises and trust His word.

BIG THOUGHT:

**Elohim is creative, strong, trustworthy, and good.
Trust Him.**

Quote to Ponder

How refreshing to know Elohim! . . . With Him all things are possible. Every promise is affirmed by His will and by His name.
LEHMAN STRAUSS[1]

Questions to Consider

1. What did you find most interesting or surprising in this discussion of Elohim?
2. Which appeals to you more: Elohim's power, His trustworthiness, or His goodness?

KNOWING GOD BY HIS NAMES

El Shaddai, God Almighty

Are you facing an impossible situation? Do you feel woefully weak and insufficient? Are you in a significant storm? Are you experiencing severe attack from the enemy?

You need to know El Shaddai.

The name *Shaddai* appears forty-eight times in the Old Testament. *El Shaddai*, which appears seven times, is a compound of two Hebrew words: *El* ("God") and *Shaddai* ("almighty"). This name, "God Almighty," reveals two primary sides of El Shaddai: He is our Source *and* Shelter.

El Shaddai: The Source, Sustainer, and Satisfaction of Life

A deeper dive into the background of this name reveals that the word *Shaddai* comes from the word Hebrew word *shad*, meaning "breast"—implying sustenance, strength, satisfaction, and sufficiency.

> *All that a mother is to her baby, El Shaddai is to His own children. He is the mighty One, the believer's Sufficiency, Sustenance, Strength, and Satisfaction. As the mother pours her life into the child of her breast, even so El Shaddai pours His life into His children.*[1]

The first time the name *El Shaddai* appears in scripture is in the story of Abraham. As you know, God promised that Abraham would have a son. For over twenty years though, nothing happened. Yet God had promised that Abraham and Sarah would have a son.

The problem was that both were past the age of childbearing, and their bodies were "dead" when it came to reproduction (Genesis 17:17; Romans 4:19–21; Hebrews 11:11). There was no way they could produce a child on their own. But the story of the Bible is that "to experience God's sufficiency one must realize his own insufficiency."[2]

God's response was to reveal His name, *El Shaddai*—God Almighty. "When Abram was ninety-nine years old, the LORD appeared to Abram and said to him, 'I am Almighty God'" (Genesis 17:1 NKJV). El Shaddai is the ultimate Author and Sustainer of Life.

Sarah, of course, miraculously became pregnant and bore a beautiful, healthy baby boy named Isaac (meaning "laughter"). El Shaddai gave an elderly couple a miracle baby (Genesis 21:2), and the child brought them such satisfaction that they named him "laughter."

El Shaddai: The Shelter and Shield of Protection

Many who have faced storms of life or seasons of intense spiritual warfare have found Psalm 91 to be a great encouragement. Although the Hebrew text mentions no author, the Greek Septuagint translation of the Old Testament attributes it to David. That makes sense—if anyone endured the brunt of brutal physical attacks, emotional setbacks, personal failures, and spiritual onslaught, it was David. Through it all, he found encouragement in the name *El Shaddai*.

> *He who dwells in the shelter of the Most High will*
> *remain secure and rest in the shadow of the Almighty*
> *[whose power no enemy can withstand].*
> PSALM 91:1 AMP

> *I will say of the LORD, "He is my refuge and my fortress [El*
> *Shaddai], My God, in whom I trust [with great confidence, and*
> *on whom I rely]!" For He will save you from the trap of the*
> *fowler, and from the deadly pestilence. He will cover you and*
> *completely protect you with His pinions, and under His wings*
> *you will find refuge; His faithfulness is a shield and a wall.*
> PSALM 91:2–4 AMP

God's Protection: You'll Need It

I have played a role in many church plants and been the point man for starting two significant churches focused on reaching the unchurched. I know from experience that when you step up for God, the enemy steps up his attacks. The harder you go for God, the harder the enemy will fight you. Make no mistake about it. You will experience spiritual attack. It comes in several forms:

DISTRESS IN THE NIGHT

Several years ago, I was speaking to a large group of missionaries who had offered themselves to reach the least reached: Hindus, Muslims, and Buddhists. At the beginning of one session I asked them, "How many of you, when you accepted the call or when you arrived on your mission field, began to have nightmares—or woke up in the night flooded with negative thoughts and anxious feelings?"

At first, only few raised their hands. But soon, there must have been more than a hundred. After the session, they lined up to talk to me and receive prayer.

I have seen the same thing with church planters, especially those in hard-to-reach places. Why? Because the enemy attacks those who are on the front lines of the Gospel.

Noted pastor and Bible teacher Charles Swindoll, when writing about Psalm 91, gave this testimony:

> My wife and I have often talked about how we can sense the invisible presence of the adversary. There are subtle yet distinct hints that evil forces are at work. There is a heaviness in one's spirit, a lingering realization that what we are dealing with is more than a human being is causing. Usually there are unexplainable coincidences and at the same time superhuman feelings of oppression that bear down on the mind. . . . There is no mistaking the source—the enemy of our souls is behind such [attacks]."[3]

I find that praying through Psalm 91 and crying out to El Shaddai before going to bed usually solves these attacks. Nightmares cease. Late-night anxiety attacks stop. Peace reigns.

DISCOURAGING OPPOSITION

Years ago, when we started our first church, I was driving to a rough part of town to visit a man named Jonathan. He had been visiting our church, and I was sure he was ready to be saved.

As I got near his house, my car—which had never given me trouble and was running fine—began to sputter. There was plenty of gas and the oil was fine.

Why is this happening? I thought.

Then it hit me. *This must be an enemy attack.*

The car kept sputtering, so I began to pray. Finally, the car stopped and would not start again. I was less than a block from Jonathan's house, so I got out, locked the doors, and walked down the street. It was very dark, and the streetlight was broken.

All the way, I prayed to El Shaddai to protect me and use me to witness to Jonathan.

Less than an hour later, Jonathan gave his life to Christ. (And he has remained faithful to Christ ever since.)

I walked back to my car, praying to El Shaddai to protect me and make the car start. When I turned the key, it started immediately and ran home like a top. I never had another problem with it.

El Shaddai had protected me—and brought eternal life to Jonathan.

DIRECT RESISTANCE

A few years ago, in mid-January, we started a church in urban Las Vegas. Our primary campus met in a middle school on Sundays. But at the end of January—on a Friday afternoon at 4:50 p.m.—a secretary with the school board called to say there were problems with our paperwork. We would not be able to meet in the school that Sunday.

Earlier in the week, we had checked our papers and everything was fine. So, we asked to speak to the woman's boss, but she said her supervisor was gone for the weekend—as was everyone else with the authority to overturn her decision. We were stuck.

It smelled like an enemy attack. We "just happened" to be

in the midst of a special twenty-one-days-of-prayer emphasis, and were holding daily prayer meetings over three weeks. So, at the meeting that night, we shared the situation and prayed for protection and wisdom. By the end of the meeting, the Lord had given us a plan: call all 175 people who came to our brand-new church to tell them we would combine a church service with a block party (with inflatables, grills, and games) and meet in the park near the school. We cried out to El Shaddai to provide and protect.

Las Vegas is usually very dry, except in January. The weather service predicted cold rain all day Saturday and Sunday, which would ruin our "church in the park" idea. Even if it only rained on Saturday, the park could be a mess on Sunday.

When we woke up Saturday, it was pouring. Several of our church members met in the park, and stood in the rain praying for the rain to stop and the wind to dry the grass. But it continued to rain all afternoon and into the evening.

It appeared as though the enemy had won. But El Shaddai is the Almighty God.

Late that night the rain stopped. A strong wind blew through the valley. By Sunday morning the sun was out and the grass in the park was dry.

El Shaddai won a great victory. We held church in the park and seven people were saved! Then we had a great block party afterward, and we were able to minister to even more people. It was amazing.

On top of that, it so happened that a prize-winning, Jewish-born, atheist writer was interviewing me for the *Las Vegas Review-Journal*. He had heard that we were feeding the homeless, reaching college students, and seeing addicts experience freedom. So he wanted to see how our church operated on Sundays. He was expecting to go to a church service in a school, so the meeting in the park (with a block party!) blew his mind.

The journalist wrote a very favorable article about us, and my picture was put on the front page of the magazine. Beyond that, he quoted my Sunday sermon in which I gave the Gospel and told people how to be saved. So 385,000 people got to read the Gospel that week!

BIG THOUGHT:

El Shaddai is the Almighty Source, Sustainer, and Satisfaction—
and our Shield against enemy attack.

Quote to Ponder

The Omnipotent Lord will shield all those who dwell with him,
they shall remain under his care as guests under the protection
of their host. . . . What a refuge in the hour of deadly storm!
Communion with God is safety.
CHARLES SPURGEON[4]

Questions to Consider

1. Which aspect of El Shaddai did you find most interesting—His being the source of life or the shelter against the enemy? Why?
2. How does knowing El Shaddai give you comfort?

DAY 10

KNOWING GOD BY HIS NAMES

El Elyon, God Most High

We all have a longing to give ourselves to that which is highest. There is something in us that compels us to acknowledge what is supreme. It makes no sense to give your life to worship a secondary god, when you can know "God Most High." His name is *El Elyon.*

The name comes from the Hebrew word, *El* ("strongest one" or "God") and *Elyon* ("the most" or "the highest"). So El Elyon is "the strongest strong One" or "the highest God."

El Elyon: The Possessor of Heaven and Earth

Early in the recorded history of Abraham, his nephew Lot—living in the wicked city of Sodom—was captured and carried away during a battle. Abraham gathered a group of 318 men to pursue the enemy army and rescue Lot. After this successful battle, Abraham met with a mysterious man named Melchizedek, "priest of God Most High" (Genesis 14:18), who pronounced a blessing over Abraham.

> *"Blessed be Abram of God Most High [El Elyon], possessor*
> *of heaven and earth; and blessed be God Most High,*
> *who has delivered your enemies into your hand."*
> GENESIS 14:19–20 NKJV

As "possessor of heaven and earth," El Elyon has rightful claim to all there is. Then Abraham offered El Elyon a tenth of his possessions (Genesis 14:20).

To know God is to acknowledge that, as El Elyon, He rightfully owns everything. We must steward our possessions as though we are managing what is ultimately His, because that is exactly the case. Like Abraham did, we must return to Him a generous portion of our income as an acknowledgment that it all comes from Him and ultimately belongs to Him.

El Elyon: The Person Whom Satan Longs to Replace

Satan hungers for power and prestige. Prior to tempting Adam and Eve in the Garden of Eden, he was the archangel, Lucifer, the "morning star, son of the dawn" (Isaiah 14:12). Satan "exercises his self-will in assaulting the authority of God and attempting to take His place."[1] In declaring the reason for Satan's ultimate downfall, God detailed His crime:

> *"You said in your heart, 'I will ascend to heaven; I will raise my throne above the stars of God; I will sit on the mount of assembly in the remote parts of the north. I will ascend above the heights of the clouds; I will make myself like the Most High [El Elyon].' "*
> Isaiah 14:13–14 AMP

Satan's lust to replace El Elyon, the Most High God, fueled his rebellion and his downfall. But he failed because, even though the devil has strength and power, El Elyon is "Almighty God" (Genesis 17:1 NKJV) and "the God of gods" (Psalm 136:2).

To know God as El Elyon is to acknowledge and submit to His deserved authority. It is to lay down our self-centered rebellion and give Him the highest place in our lives.

El Elyon: The Person Who Has a Purpose in Our Adversity

David was alone, hiding in a cave.

Insane King Saul had been chasing him around the wilderness, hoping to kill him.

It would have been a perfect time for David to whine and complain. It would seem an appropriate time for him to have a lapse of faith.

But instead, David knew God by the name of El Elyon—and he believed that the Most High would answer his prayers. David also believed that the crazy, awful season of suffering in which he found himself was part of a larger plan and a greater purpose. Listen to his confident prayer:

> I call to God Most High, to God who fulfills his purpose for me.
> Psalm 57:2 CSB

To know God as El Elyon is to remain true to Him in adversity, trusting that He will ultimately fulfill His will for your life.

El Elyon: The Person to Whom World Leaders Must Bow

The book of the Bible which uses the name El Elyon most frequently is Daniel. As you may recall, when Jerusalem was crushed by the Babylonians around 606 BC, the victors carried the spoils of Israel—including high-potential young men—back to Babylon. Such men included Daniel and his three friends, Shadrach, Meshach, and Abednego.

The first section of Daniel illustrates how El Elyon is greater than the greatest kings of the greatest nation on earth, that El Elyon is superior to their gods, and that El Elyon alone is the Most High God, possessor of heaven and earth. The last section of Daniel shows that El Elyon is greater than the greatest world powers of all time, and that, ultimately, *everyone* must bow before the Most High God.

Let's look at these truths in more detail.

El Elyon and the Execution Furnace (Daniel 3)

King Nebuchadnezzar was the most powerful man in the greatest nation on earth. His capital, Babylon, was unrivaled in wealth and beauty. Herodotus, a historian in 450 BC, wrote that Babylon surpassed every city in the known world in its splendor.

During his long reign, King Nebuchadnezzar constructed an astonishing array of temples, palaces, walls, and gardens. His mountainous terraces, the "hanging gardens," were so stunning in beauty and in architecture that they have been acclaimed as one of the seven wonders of the ancient world.

Nebuchadnezzar decided he had achieved the lofty status of a god. So he had a giant gold statue made in his likeness to proudly proclaim his glory. Then Nebuchadnezzar ordered the important officials in his kingdom to come and bow before the ninety-foot-tall image—or die.

Shadrach, Meshach, and Abednego, Daniel's friends, were unbelievably fearless and resolute. They believed El Elyon was greater than all other gods.

> Shadrach, Meshach and Abed-nego replied to the king,
> "O Nebuchadnezzar, we do not need to give you an answer
> concerning this matter. If it be so, our God whom we serve
> is able to deliver us from the furnace of blazing fire; and He
> will deliver us out of your hand, O king. But even if He does not,
> let it be known to you, O king, that we are not going to serve
> your gods or worship the golden image that you have set up."
> DANIEL 3:16–18 NASB

Obviously, such bold declarations were not what Nebuchadnezzar wanted to hear. Incensed, he ordered the execution furnace heated to seven times its normal temperature. It was so incredibly hot that it killed the guards who dropped the three men down into the furnace. The three Hebrews would surely catch fire like dry kindling and be consumed in minutes.

But as Nebuchadnezzar peered into the furnace, he did not expect what he saw. Shocked and stunned, he turned to his advisors and asked,

> "Weren't there three men that we tied up and threw into the
> fire?" They replied, "Certainly, Your Majesty." He said, "Look!
> I see four men walking around in the fire, unbound and un-
> harmed, and the fourth looks like a son of the gods."
> DANIEL 3:24–25

He got it all correct, except the last part. Yes, the men were all alive. Yes, they were now unbound. Yes, they were unharmed.

Yes, there was a fourth in the fire. But the fourth was not merely "like a son of the gods." He *was* the Son of God! Jesus, the ultimate King of kings, went with them through the fire.

But that's not all. Shadrach, Meshach, and Abednego not only walked out unharmed, they didn't even smell of smoke (Daniel 3:27)! Nebuchadnezzar was so impressed that he called them "servants of the Most High God" (Daniel 3:26). The king decreed that no one could speak against the God of Shadrach, Meshach, and Abednego (Daniel 3:28–29), and he gave the men a promotion (Daniel 3:30).

EL ELYON AND THE MANIACAL KING (DANIEL 4)

Unfortunately, the proud Nebuchadnezzar still did not bow his knees and will to the Most High God. So, El Elyon gave the king a troubling dream of his future, "in order that the living may know that the Most High rules in the kingdom of men" (Daniel 4:17 NKJV).

Daniel interpreted the king's dream with a warning that the king needed to repent. But the arrogant Nebuchadnezzar refused. Therefore, the dream was fulfilled: insanity visited the stubborn king, and he lived as a maniac in the wilderness. Finally, the king humbled himself and repented saying:

> "I blessed the Most High and praised and honored Him who lives forever: For His dominion is an everlasting dominion, and His kingdom is from generation to generation. All the inhabitants of the earth are reputed as nothing; He does according to His will in the army of heaven and among the inhabitants of the earth. No one can restrain His hand or say to Him, "What have You done?"
> DANIEL 4:34–35 NKJV

At this, his sanity returned, and his kingdom was restored.

> Now I, Nebuchadnezzar, praise and extol and honor the King of heaven, all of whose works are truth, and His ways justice. And those who walk in pride He is able to put down.
> DANIEL 4:37 NKJV

When you really think about it, failing to bow to the Most High God may be the ultimate insanity.

To Know El Elyon

To know El Elyon is to acknowledge that He is the sovereign ruler of the universe and the One to whom we must bow. Therefore, we should give Him every aspect of our lives—including our family, health, job, finances, possessions, future, past, dreams, and doubts.

To know God as El Elyon is to acknowledge and submit to His deserved authority. It is to lay down our self-centered rebellion and give Him the highest place in our lives.

To know God as El Elyon is to acknowledge that He rightfully owns everything. It is to remain true to Him in adversity, trusting that He will ultimately fulfill His will for our lives.

BIG THOUGHT:

El Elyon is the Most High God.
Bow before Him, give Him the highest
place in your life, and trust Him.

Quote to Ponder

> El Elyon is "the strongest strong One." None is
> greater as He in power or possessions.
> LEHMAN STRAUSS[2]

Questions to Consider

1. Which of the portraits of El Elyon means the most to you?
   - ☐ The possessor of heaven and earth?
   - ☐ The person Satan longs to replace?
   - ☐ The person who has a purpose in your adversity?
   - ☐ The person to whom world leaders must bow?
2. Which response do you most need to apply?
   - ☐ Dedicate your possessions to Him?
   - ☐ Bow humbly before Him?
   - ☐ Trust Him to fulfill His purposes in your adversity?

KNOWING GOD BY HIS NAMES

YHWH, the Great I AM

Imagine discovering a beautiful, leather-bound book. You open it to find that it contains hundreds of checks. But unlike any other checkbook you have ever seen, each check is already made out . . .to you.

Then your curious eyes fall on the "amount" section. Goose bumps break out all over your arms when you see what is written. One of them says, "Peace"; the next, "Victory"; the one after that, "Guidance"; and the next says, "Strength." They offer amazing blessings for your emotional, spiritual, and practical life.

This must be a joke, you think. *This cannot be true.*

Slowly, almost fearfully, your eyes move down to the lower right-hand corner to see who signed these checks guaranteeing so many blessings. Interestingly, each check has already been endorsed by the same person: "YHWH." You are staggered by the reality that this is no joke.

YHWH: Jehovah, I AM

More than three thousand years ago, the Lord strategically placed a newborn Hebrew baby, Moses, in the household of Egypt's pharaoh. Ultimately, Moses was one day to rescue the enslaved Israelites and lead them to the Promised Land. But Moses ran ahead of God and got himself in trouble: he ended up fleeing for his life into the wilderness of Midian.

For forty years, the fugitive thought he was hiding from God. But God knew exactly where Moses was. And when Moses was ready to be useful, the Lord commandeered a bush, set it ablaze with His presence, and called him through the strange, miraculous object. It was time for Moses to fulfill his purpose.

But the seemingly impossible task caused Moses to shrink back in fear and hopelessness.

> *Moses said to God, "Who am I that I should go to Pharaoh, and that I should bring the children of Israel out of Egypt?"*
> Exodus 3:11 NKJV

Moses utterly missed the point, thinking his assignment was all about who *he* was. But Moses was wrong. The big issue in life is not "who *we* are," but rather, "who *God* is."

Let me repeat that: the big issue in life is not who we are, but rather, who God is.

You will never really know yourself *until* you know God. You will only deeply know yourself *to the extent that* you deeply know God.

What did God say to alleviate Moses' fear and apprehension?

> *"I will certainly be with you. And this shall be a sign to you that I have sent you: When you have brought the people out of Egypt, you shall serve God on this mountain."*
> *Then Moses said to God, "Indeed, when I come to the children of Israel and say to them, 'The God of your fathers has sent me to you,' and they say to me, 'What is His name?' what shall I say to them?"*
> *And God said to Moses, "I AM WHO I AM." And He said, "Thus you shall say to the children of Israel, 'I AM [YHWH] has sent me to you.'"*
> Exodus 3:12–14 NKJV

The Lord revealed Himself to Moses with the unusual name of "I AM WHO I AM" (Hebrew: YHWH). Everything we will ever need is found in that name. Simply put, "I AM" means that "God is" exactly what we need. The name is "unfinished" in part to allow us to put after it what we need. Therefore, we should run to Him, not to other things, to meet our needs.

In her classic book *The God of All Comfort*, Hannah Whitall Smith discussed the transforming, practical encouragement available to us through the name of Yahweh:

> God tells us through all the pages of His Book what He is. "I am," He says, "all that my people need"; "I am their strength"; "I am their wisdom"; "I am their righteousness"; "I am their peace"; "I am their salvation"; "I am their life"; "I am their all in all." This apparently unfinished name, therefore, is the most comforting name the heart of man could devise, because it allows us to add to it, without any limitation, whatever we feel the need of, and even exceeding abundantly beyond all that we can ask or think.[1]

YHWH

Here are several quick facts about YHWH:

1. YHWH is the most personal and most popular name of God in the Bible, with some sixty-eight hundred references in the Old Testament.
2. YHWH is the most important name for God in the Old Testament.
3. YHWH is a name that our English versions render with all capital letters, as "Lord."
4. YHWH means "self-existing"—He is the one who never came into being, and the one who always will be.
5. YHWH is the most intensely sacred name to Jewish scribes, and many will not even pronounce it.
6. YHWH is sometimes pronounced as "Jehovah"—that was an attempt to pronounce the consonants Y-H-W-H.

YHWH, Jehovah, the I AM

"I AM" is a simple little name that is loaded with massive, mind-shattering ramifications. Here are some more quick facts about *YHWH, Jehovah, the I AM*.

1. When God revealed Himself as "I AM," He was stating that He alone is *self-existent and eternal*. Jehovah had no

beginning and He will never end. Since He did not come into being, He cannot go out of being, because He *is* being. He is the only one who can say, "I AM, and I have always been and always will be."

2. When God revealed Himself as "I AM," He was stating that He is the lone being in the universe who is *self-sufficient*. He said: "I AM, and I caused all else to be." He is the cause of all, but is caused by none. He alone is the great Uncaused Cause.

3. When God revealed Himself as "I AM," He was stating that He alone is *utterly independent*. He depended on nothing to bring Him into being and depends on nothing to sustain Himself.

4. When God revealed Himself as "I AM," He indicated that He is the *ultimate source*. He exists without any help from anyone or anything else. He is the only entity in the universe with no needs. Therefore, He is free to meet our needs. When God described Himself as "I AM," He was saying, "I existed before your need and will exist after your need." He does not depend upon anything else, but everything else depends upon Him. The entire universe came into being *by God* and remains moment by moment *because of God*.

5. When God revealed Himself as "I AM," He was stating that He is *constant*. He was saying, "I AM, and I always will be exactly all that I AM." He is the same yesterday, today, and forever (Hebrews 13:8). Because God is complete and perfect in all ways, He cannot be improved upon, and does not need to change.

Add all these things together and you will discover one final, ultimate, awesome thing it means when God declared His name to be "I AM":

When God revealed Himself as "I AM," He was stating that He is—right this very moment—*exactly what we need*.

For the next forty years, Moses discovered that Jehovah was

everything he needed: wisdom, guidance, strength, hope, power, provision, and help. Moses found Jehovah to be like a blank check, the personal provision of *everything* he needed.

Elsewhere in the Old Testament, when God's people were in need, we see the name *Jehovah* combined with other words to remind us how God meets our needs:

- *Jehovah Jireh*, the LORD Who Sees and Provides (Genesis 22:14)
- *Jehovah Nissi*, the LORD My Banner [of Victory] (Exodus 17:15)
- *Jehovah Shalom*, the LORD of Peace (Judges 6:24)
- *Jehovah Roi*, the Lord My Shepherd (Psalm 23:1)
- *Jehovah Sabaoth*, the Lord of Angel Armies (1 Samuel 17:45)
- *Jehovah Ozi*, the Lord My Strength (2 Samuel 22:33)
- *Jehovah Tsidkenu*, the Lord Our Righteousness (Jeremiah 23:5–6)
- *Jehovah Mekaddishkem*, the Lord Our Sanctifier—the One who sets us apart and makes us holy (Exodus 31:12–13)

Because "He Is," We Are...

An old story states that while praying one day, a woman asked, "Who are you, God?"

He answered, "I AM."

"But who is I AM?" the woman asked.

He replied, "I Am Love. I Am Peace. I Am Grace. I Am Joy. I Am Strength. I Am the Creator. I Am the Comforter. I Am the Beginning and the End. I Am the Way, Truth, and the Life."

With tears in her eyes, the woman looked toward heaven and said, "Now I understand—

but who am I?"

God tenderly wiped the tears from her eyes and whispered, "You are Mine."

To Know YHWH

To know God as YHWH is to recognize that everything you need is in Him. As we follow Jehovah's direction, we will find Him to be—just like Moses did—a blank check, the personal provision of everything we need.

BIG THOUGHT:

YHWH, Jehovah, and the "I AM" all mean that "God is" exactly what we need. Therefore, we should run to Him, not to other things, to meet our needs.

Quote to Ponder

The significance of the name Jehovah is, in its revelation of God, becoming to His people what they need in order to supply that need.
LEHMAN STRAUSS[2]

Questions to Consider

1. Which of the facts about YHWH do you find most interesting?
2. Which of the Jehovah-combination names do you find most important to you right now?

KNOWING GOD BY HIS NAMES

Jehovah Roi, the LORD, My Shepherd

Let's play a game. What animal comes to mind when I say the following?

- fierce fighter
- blazing speed
- razor-sharp claws
- camouflaged coat
- keen, cunning craftiness
- terrifying roar

Did you answer "sheep" to all of those descriptions? Did you answer "sheep" to *any* of the descriptions?

You probably answered "no" to all of my questions, because sheep are essentially defenseless and helpless. Their fluffy white coat is not good camouflage. Their dull teeth and hooves pose no threat to a predator. They are slow. Their *baa* does not scare anyone. And they are dumb.

If sheep get caught in a fast-running stream, the weight of the water in their wool will pull them under—and they will drown. Sheep only lie down when their stomachs are filled and, once down, might need help to get up. Of all animals, they are most dependent on help—a good shepherd.

No wonder the Bible calls *us* sheep.

No wonder David called God by the name *Jehovah Roi*, the LORD, My Shepherd.

The LORD is my shepherd.
PSALM 23:1 NKJV

Note that *LORD* is in capital letters, indicating that this is the name *Yahweh* and not *Adonai* (which we'll discuss in greater detail on Day 14). And note that the verb *is* is treated differently here—because it is not in the original Hebrew text but was inserted by translators. I prefer that the *is* not be added so the name of God stands clear: "The LORD, My Shepherd."

Elmer Towns writes that Psalm 23 contains several descriptions of the shepherding ministry of God for His people, descriptions that can be linked with other Jehovah names of scripture:

The LORD is my shepherd;	*Jehovah Roi*, the LORD, My Shepherd
I shall not want. He makes	
me to lie down in green pastures;	*Jehovah Jireh*, the LORD [Our] Provider
He leads me beside the still waters.	*Jehovah Shalom*, the LORD [Our] Peace
He restores my soul;	*Jehovah Rapha*, the LORD [Our] Healer
He leads me in paths of righteousness	
For His name's sake.	*Jehovah Tsidkenu*, the LORD [Our] Righteousness
Yea, though I walk through the valley	
of the shadow of death,	
I will fear no evil;	*Jehovah Nissi*, the LORD [Our] Banner of Victory
For You are with me.	*Jehovah Shammah*, the LORD Is Present[1]

Remember that God is a whole being. Each of His attributes works in concert with all the others. Each of His names work in union with the others. All of them combine to make Him the Great Shepherd.

Jehovah Roi, the LORD, My Shepherd and *Jehovah Jireh*, the LORD, [Our] Provider.

A few years ago, my older brother Steve was battling lung cancer. At the time, Cathy and I were living in Las Vegas, leading a group of ministries called Grace City. I had a crazy schedule, but I really wanted to see Steve. But he was living near Columbus, Ohio.

I was traveling a great deal, speaking in churches to raise money for the Las Vegas ministries as well as recruiting college students to help us. One Friday night, Cathy and I were hoping to make a flight from the East Coast across country to Las Vegas. But because of bad weather and airline issues, our initial flight into Charlotte was late. As we ran through the airport trying to catch our plane to Las Vegas, I happened to notice a screen showing a 10:20 p.m. flight to Columbus.

By the time we reached the gate, our flight from Charlotte to Las Vegas had been canceled. So we lined up to try to get a flight back to Las Vegas the next day, but the airline people were no help, all the flights were full, and all the hotels were booked. It looked like we were going to have to spend the night in the airport before trying it all again the next day.

I suddenly felt an overwhelming desire to see my brother. Cathy and I really needed Jehovah Roi and Jehovah Jireh, the LORD, [Our] Shepherd and Provider to help us.

Then, I just happened to remember seeing that late-night flight to Columbus, Ohio. Two seats just happened to have opened up on that plane. We just happened to be re-routed to Las Vegas through Columbus. We just happened to have enough time to run through the airport again and get on that flight.

In Columbus the next morning, I drove downtown to the James Cancer Hospital to see my brother for what turned out to be the last time. Two weeks later, he died.

The Good Shepherd knew all about that, of course, and He came through for us. Jehovah Jireh provided an unexpected trip to Columbus. Jehovah Roi shepherded us through the situation.

Jehovah Roi, the Lord, My Shepherd and *Jehovah Nissi*, the Lord, [Our] Banner of Victory

Thirty years ago, outside of Columbus, Ohio, Cathy and I started a church in a school. The board set a limit for how long they would allow us to rent the school, and then we'd have to move out. Our church was growing very quickly, and we had outgrown every other possible meeting place in the city. So we needed to buy land and try to get zoning approval to put up a church building.

I had met with everyone in the neighborhood and listened to their concerns, which were few. We adjusted our zoning proposal to satisfy their needs, and I thought everything was set for approval.

The night of the zoning meeting, I was sick with a severe stomach virus. But I went to the meeting anyway, certain the zoning committee would give its approval.

I was wrong. I walked into a hornet's nest.

The room was full of angry neighbors. One woman who did not live in the neighborhood (but who had strong political aspirations) had gone in after me, rallying our neighbors to oppose the building of a church.

The zoning committee heard our neighbors issue a list of complaints they had not shared with me. Then I was given two weeks to create a new plan that addressed all the concerns. At that meeting, a final vote would be held.

I went home feeling extremely discouraged. I needed Jehovah Nissi, *the Lord, My Banner of Victory*.

Throughout the next week, I went back and met one-by-one with each of the neighbors and city officials involved. Then I went back to our architect and got an updated plan. The zoning officials called to remind me that I had only one more shot at getting approval, and that would be at the upcoming meeting.

I explained the opposition to our church membership, and they began to pray against this spiritual attack. Then I invited our people to pack out the zoning committee room, and to pray while I made the presentation. All week long, I prayed too.

Jehovah Nissi, we are dealing with someone with an anti-church agenda, someone trying to block our church from being built in that needy neighborhood. Years ago, You gave the Egyptians plagues. I humbly ask that on the night of the zoning meeting, You give that lady a stomach virus much worse than the one I had last time.

On the night of the meeting, I walked into a room filled with people. There were one hundred seats in the room, and one hundred people from our church had showed up.

The neighborhood agitator was not in the room. The lone representative for the neighbors said that the lady had called to say she was too sick to attend. . . .

Our proposal passed with flying colors. Yay, God!

The Good Shepherd came through. Jehovah Roi shepherded us through the situation and gave us victory. When you are doing God's thing, *God* is your victory!

Jesus Is Our Good Shepherd

Jesus is the embodiment of the heart and ministry of a "good shepherd." He explained His role as life-giving, sacrificial, committed, caring, and personal. And Jesus described His relationship with His sheep as intimate—enough for Him to know our names and for us to know His voice. Jesus even said that our relationship with Him could be as intimate as His own relationship with His Father.

> *"I am the good shepherd; I know my sheep and my sheep know me—just as the Father knows me and I know the Father—and I lay down my life for the sheep."*
> JOHN 10:14–15

> *"My sheep listen to my voice; I know them, and they follow me."*
> JOHN 10:27

The author of Hebrews referred to Jesus as the "great Shepherd" (Hebrews 13:20). The apostle Peter called Him "the Shepherd and Guardian of your souls" (1 Peter 2:25 NASB) and "the Chief Shepherd" (1 Peter 5:4).

Knowing God as Jehovah Roi

When he wrote, "The Lord is my shepherd" (Psalm 23:1), David took God's shepherding ministry personally. Being shepherded by the Lord is the result of having a personal faith relationship with Him. Therefore, if you have not trusted Jesus as your Savior, it begins there.

If you have trusted Jesus as your Savior, learn to trust Him as your Shepherd too. Realize that, in many ways, you are a helpless sheep—desperately in need of His protection, direction, correction, and provision.

Trust Him.

BIG THOUGHT:

The Lord is the Great Shepherd.
Therefore, trust Him to guard you, guide you,
and provide you with everything you truly need.

Quote to Ponder

The Eastern shepherd was the guide of his flock. The sheep never thought of going before him—it would have been an anomaly in nature for the sheep to go first, and for the shepherd to follow. They had no need whatever to know the way across the trackless desert—it was enough for them that the shepherd knew it.
C. H. Spurgeon[2]

Questions to Consider

1. How does seeing the Lord as your Shepherd comfort you and make it easier to trust Him?
2. Where do you need to trust the Good Shepherd right now?

KNOWING GOD BY HIS NAMES

Jehovah Jireh, the LORD Our Provider

Have you ever tried to do God's will in God's way, and still found yourself in serious need?

Remember these two truths: First, you aren't alone. Second, God's got a name for that.

Jehovah Jireh: I AM...Your Provider

The Hebrew word *Jireh* comes from the root word "to see" and speaks of "seeing to a matter, providing." As we strive to obey God, He sees our needs and acts to meet them.

The name *Jehovah Jireh* comes from an incident in the life of Abraham. In Genesis 22, God put Abraham's faith to the supreme test: the Lord asked Abraham to offer his son Isaac as a sacrifice. Sometimes we become so familiar with a story that its true impact escapes us. Think about this sacrifice that God commanded:

- Isaac was Abraham's *son*.
- Isaac was a true *miracle*. Both Sarah (age ninety) and Abraham (age ninety-nine) were much too old to produce children when Isaac was conceived.
- Isaac was the focal point of God's covenant with Abraham. When Abraham met God, he was named *Abram*, which means "father." Yet he had no children. Then God changed Abram's name to *Abraham* ("father of many"). God promised that through Abraham's seed would come a great nation. Isaac was the fulfillment of that promise, the one whom God promised to make into a mighty nation.

When God told Abraham to offer up his son, Isaac, He was demanding the supreme sacrifice. I am sure that Abraham would gladly have traded anything else, including his own life.

Yet, in a wonderful display of faith, obedience, and worship, Abraham took the boy up the mountain to sacrifice him. How it must have pained Abraham when Isaac asked, "Look, the fire and the wood, but where is the lamb for a burnt offering?" (Genesis 22:7 NKJV).

Abraham responded with tremendous faith in Jehovah Jireh. "My son," he answered, "God will provide for Himself the lamb for a burnt offering" (Genesis 22:8 NKJV). Abraham is lauded as a man of faith because he believed in God's provision *before* God provided.

Abraham went on and built an altar, then tied Isaac down and raised his knife to sacrifice him. (Now, if the idea of human sacrifice troubles you—as it should—remember that God was not really after Isaac's life. He really wanted Abraham's heart.)

Fortunately, an angel of the Lord stopped Abraham before he could hurt Isaac. Then Abraham "just happened" to discover a ram, caught in a thicket by its horns. So he offered the ram instead of Isaac as his offering to the Lord. Abraham worshipped God, calling the name of the place "The-LORD-Will-Provide" (Genesis 22:14 NKJV).

Jehovah Jireh provided.

It is interesting to note that Abraham did not say that Jehovah had provided in the past, or that He is providing in the present—rather that Jehovah *will* provide, in the future. We now know that the future provision (from Abraham's perspective) would be the ultimate sacrifice, God's own Son. Jesus, the Lamb of God, would serve as payment for the sins of the world (John 1:29).

For his faith-filled obedience to God's Word and abandonment to God's will, Abraham was provided for. When you are trying to do God's will in God's way, God will provide.

Trust, Not Worry

The apostle Paul also found that when you are trying to do God's will in God's way, God will provide. In his letter to the church at Philippi, he commanded the people to turn their worries into prayerful petitions: "Do not be anxious about anything, but in every situation, by prayer and petition, with thanksgiving, present your requests to God" (Philippians 4:6).

Then, after thanking the Philippians for providing for his needs as a missionary, he gave them a precious promise: "My God will meet all your needs according to the riches of his glory in Christ Jesus" (Philippians 4:19).

And Jesus Himself taught that when you are trying to do God's will, God's way, God will provide. First, He commanded us to not worry: "I tell you, do not worry about your life, what you will eat or drink; or about your body, what you will wear" (Matthew 6:25). Jesus said that worrying about such things makes us no different than people who don't know our heavenly Father (Matthew 6:28–32), and that the core of worry is unbelief: "you of little faith" (Matthew 6:30). Instead of worrying, Jesus said we should focus our lives on God and how we can partner with Him in advancing His kingdom: "But seek first his kingdom and his righteousness, and all these things will be given to you as well" (Matthew 6:33).

I AM. . .Your Provider

Some might think, *Well, that all sounds good. . .but how can I know that God will provide for* me? Allow me to offer several examples from my own experience.

THE BANK ACCOUNT

I had a great situation at Liberty University: I was chair of my department and director of the Center for Ministry Training. Good paychecks, a great retirement plan, and strong health insurance were part of the deal. Cathy and I owned a beautiful house in the country, one with a spectacular view of the Blue Ridge Mountains. But in order to start a church in Las Vegas, Nevada, we had to leave all of that behind and trust Jehovah to provide.

Cathy and I made a commitment not to take a paycheck from the church. As we tried to do God's thing, God's way, we received zero dollars from anyone in Las Vegas. We were supported missionaries living on gifts that other people sent us.

We served in Las Vegas for four years and, at the end of each year, we had *more* money in our bank account than when we started the church.

I know. It does not make sense. But money came in from unexpected sources, time after time.

Jehovah Jireh provided. When you are trying to do God's will, God's way, God will provide.

THE FOOD DID NOT RUN OUT

While we were ministering in Las Vegas, God gave my son Andrew an incredible ministry to street people. Once a week, Andrew filled up his apartment with guys off the street for a meal and Bible study. Within a few months the group had outgrown Andrew's apartment, so the ministry moved to the park.

The first night there, Andrew and a few others prepared food for twenty-five. Nearly fifty poor, hungry people showed up to eat and study the Bible. Yet, miraculously, the food did not run out. Everyone got their fill.

The next week, Andrew's team fixed food for fifty, but over seventy-five people showed up. Yet the food never ran out until everyone had eaten.

The third week, food was prepared for seventy-five people. Over one hundred came and were fed.

Jehovah Jireh provided. When you are trying to do God's will, God's way, God will provide.

ONE HUNDRED THOUSAND DOLLARS

Andrew and the homeless group continued to draw big crowds to the park for the weekly meal and Bible study. Other people heard what was going on and began bringing clothes and supplies for distribution to the needy to Andrew's apartment. Soon, so many donations were arriving that the apartment was full.

We decided to rent a building and turn it into a weekday outreach center. A businessman in Columbus, Ohio, told us to find a place to lease for about thirty-five thousand dollars a year, and he and a friend would pay the rent.

So we found a place.

A few weeks later, on the day the lease was to be signed, Andrew called the businessman to confirm. The man hemmed and hawed, eventually saying he would not be able to fulfill his commitment.

Andrew called me, asking, "Dad, what should I do?"

I said, "God had been providing for us all along the way. It is obvious that He is doing amazing things with our homeless ministry. So, it may ruin your credit, but sign the lease."

After we hung up, I thought, *What have I done? Where are we going to get thirty-five thousand dollars to pay that rent? Andrew's funds are insufficient and so are mine.*

Then I remembered, "*Jehovah Jireh*: YHWH says, I AM your provider!"

A couple of hours later, my phone rang.

It was the pastor of a large church where I had spoken several months earlier. He and his wife had asked me a million questions about our ministry, especially about the street people and the homeless. The pastor had told me that he had connections with a foundation that gave grants "for those sort of things," and to send him a one-page proposal listing various needs and their costs.

So I had sent him a document that listed several levels of opportunity, from a total of five thousand dollars all the way up to one hundred thousand dollars. I had sent it to the pastor months earlier, and forgotten all about it.

Jehovah Jireh did not forget.

On the phone, the pastor told me, "I want you to know that our foundation approved the proposal you sent me about the homeless."

"Really?" I asked stunned.

"Yes."

"How much did they approve?" I asked eagerly. I was expecting him to say five thousand, or maybe even ten thousand dollars.

"One hundred thousand dollars," he replied. "Will that work?"

Ah, let me think. . . . "Yes!"

"Good," he said. "We'll send the check next week."

Jehovah Jireh provided. The money allowed us to do everything we needed to open the center *and* buy two mini-buses to pick up people for services. When you are trying to do God's will, God's way, God will provide.

Knowing God as Jehovah Jireh

To know God as Jehovah Jireh, trust Him to provide everything you need to obey Him. Spend your energies obeying God rather than scheming how you can meet the needs. Knowing God as Jehovah Jireh means you do not obsessively think about, talk about, or worry about provision. It means you obey God and trust Him to provide.

BIG THOUGHT:

The Lord promises to be our provider when we step out to do His will. Trust Him.

Quote to Consider

Don't take the pressure of your provision upon yourself. It is not only wrong to worry, it is unbelief; worrying means we do not believe that God can look after the practical details of our lives, and it is never anything but those details that worry us.
OSWALD CHAMBERS[1]

Questions to Ponder

1. On a scale of 1 to 3, with 1 being "little faith" and 3 being "strong faith," where do you fall?
2. Where is the Lord calling you to obey and trust that He will provide?

DAY 14

KNOWING GOD BY HIS NAMES

Adonai, Lord and Master

We live in the age of entitlement. "Claim your rights." "Stand up for yourself." "They owe you." "You deserve better." These are the battle cries of our culture.

These slogans also stand in opposition to real Christianity.

Notice how the apostle Paul identified himself in his letter to the Romans:

> *Paul,* a bondservant of Jesus Christ, *called to be an apostle, separated to the gospel of God...*
> ROMANS 1:1 NKJV, EMPHASIS ADDED

Paul authored half the books of the New Testament. He was one of the greatest missionary church planters in history. He was arguably the most influential man born after Jesus Christ. Yet he chose to identify himself as "a bondservant of Jesus Christ." Of all the ways Paul could have described himself—*apostle, ambassador, saint, missionary, church planter, author, disciple, rabbi, revolutionary*—he selected "bondservant of Jesus Christ." Paul repeated the description in his letters to the church at Philippi (1:1) and to Titus (1:1).

And Paul was not alone in finding his identity in his Master. Many of the most powerful men of early Christianity—James, Peter, Jude, and John—had the same perspective, and used the same title for themselves (James 1:1; 2 Peter 1:1; Jude 1:1; Revelation 1:1).

These men knew God and chose to acknowledge His lordship

in their lives. They gave their entire lives to Him. This is the way to worship God as *Adonai*.

Adonai: Lord and Master

The word *Adonai* is used 430 times in the Old Testament. It is rendered as "Lord" in our English Bibles, as opposed to *Yahweh*, which is rendered with all capital letters as "LORD." Adonai corresponds to the New Testament word for Lord, which is *Kurios*. Adonai means "Master," and expresses the personal relationship between a master and his slave.

Robert Lightner points out the importance of knowing God as Adonai:

> *There are two principles which apply to the relationship between the slave and his lord or master. The first is that the master has the right to absolute obedience from the slave. . . . The second principle is the fact that the slave has a right to expect provision and direction from his master.*[1]

Adonai Deserves Worship and Obedience

The idea of "master and slave" is offensive to many people—after all, why should any human being claim to own another? But God is so much more than a human being. He deserves absolute allegiance from each of us.

1. Adonai is our Master because He made us

Jeremiah was a major prophetic figure in the history of Israel. He authored the books of Jeremiah and Lamentations, and probably 1 and 2 Kings. Popularly known as "the weeping prophet," he obeyed the Lord even when that stance was unpopular and costly. This was because he knew that Adonai was his Creator and, therefore, his Master.

> *"Ah, Lord [Adonai] GOD! Behold, You have made the heavens and the earth by Your great power and outstretched arm. There is nothing too hard for You."*
> JEREMIAH 32:17 NKJV

2. ADONAI IS OUR MASTER BECAUSE HE IS ENTHRONED AS SUPREME RULER OVER THE UNIVERSE

Isaiah was another young prophet in Israel. Like Jeremiah, he had the courage to speak an unpopular message. Isaiah's bravery came because he had been given a vision of Adonai seated on His throne, ruling the universe (Isaiah 6:1).

The vision led Isaiah to a place of brokenhearted repentance (6:5). It also brought him to the place of willing obedience. When Adonai asked for a messenger, Isaiah gladly volunteered.

> I heard the voice of the Lord, saying: "Whom shall I send, and who will go for Us?" Then I said, "Here am I! Send me."
> ISAIAH 6:8 NKJV

3. ADONAI IS OUR MASTER BECAUSE HE DIED FOR US

The New Testament equivalent of the word *Adonai* is *Lord*. Jesus gladly accepted this title because He is "Lord of all" (Acts 10:36), "Lord of heaven and earth" (Acts 17:24), "Lord of both the dead and the living" (Romans 14:9), "Lord of glory" (1 Corinthians 2:8), and "Lord of lords" (Revelation 19:16). Jesus earned the title by laying aside the superpowers of deity, becoming a man, living a sinless life, and then dying for our sins—in our place—on the cross (Philippians 2:6–11).

Adonai Will Guide and Provide for You

Since New Testament times, Christians have been privileged to have God's own Spirit living within them, guiding and providing for our needs. But Old Testament believers knew they could call upon Adonai for the same kind of help.

NEHEMIAH

Nehemiah understood the Master relationship well. As a Hebrew slave in the land of Babylon, he had risen through the ranks to reach the status as wine-taster for the king.

When news reached Nehemiah that the tiny remnant of Jews still in Jerusalem were suffering because they had no wall to protect them, his heart was broken. Nehemiah realized that the Lord had strategically placed him in an important position in the king's cabinet—and that he could use his position to help the Jews rebuild their wall.

So Nehemiah cried out to Adonai, asking Him for favor—and the king's permission to leave his post, return to Jerusalem, and rebuild the wall.

> *"Lord [Adonai], let your ear be attentive to the prayer of this your servant and to the prayer of your servants who delight in revering your name. Give your servant success today by granting him favor in the presence of this man."*
> NEHEMIAH 1:11

THE PSALMS

The writers of the psalms viewed Adonai as the One to approach in prayer. He is both willing and able to respond to our cries to Him. In each of the following passages, "Lord" is *Adonai*:

> *Praise be to the Lord, to God our Savior,*
> *who daily bears our burdens.*
> PSALM 68:19

> *When I was in distress, I sought the Lord.*
> PSALM 77:2

> *Be merciful to me, O Lord, for I cry to You all day long.*
> *Rejoice the soul of Your servant, for to You, O Lord, I lift*
> *up my soul. For You, Lord, are good, and ready to forgive,*
> *and abundant in mercy to all those who call upon You.*
> PSALM 86:3–5 NKJV

> *Lord, hear my voice! Let Your ears be attentive*
> *to the voice of my supplications.*
> PSALM 130:2 NKJV

"Getting Your Ear Pierced" for Adonai

Paul, James, Peter, Jude, and John were the most powerful men in early Christianity. But their power came from their submission to Jesus as Lord. They choose to become His slaves—as we've already seen, each described himself as "a bondservant of Jesus Christ."

In the first century, bondservants were at the lowest scale of servitude. They were like a piece of property. Their person, and everything about them, was completely owned by their master.

The bondservant's identity was not in what he owned, but in the one who owned him. Paul and the others found their identity in the fact that they were owned by the Lord Jesus Christ. And they accepted the reality that Jesus did not *owe* them anything, He *owned* them. As a result, they owed Him everything. As bondservants, they had no will of their own, but lived their lives fulfilling the will of their Master.

Unlike other first-century slaves, bondservants were not slaves by birth or by force, but by *choice*.

> There was a law among the Hebrews that for sore poverty or debt or crime one man might become the servant of another, but he could not be held in servitude beyond a certain period. At the end of six years he must be allowed to go free (Exod. xxi. 1–6; Deut. xv. 12–17.) But if he loved his master and preferred to remain with him as his slave, then the master, in the presence of judges was to place the man against a door or doorpost and bore a hole through his ear, and this was to be the mark that he was his master's servant forever.[2]

In other words, for the bondservant, the steel-pierced ear was a symbol of a love-pierced heart. For Paul and the other New Testament leaders, being a bondservant of Jesus was the result of the spiritual piercing of their hearts and wills. They viewed themselves as bondservants of Jesus by choice, out of love for Him.

Interestingly, Paul wrote that Jesus Himself was the ultimate example of a bondservant. He willingly became a slave and obeyed the will of the Father, to the point of death.

*Think of yourselves the way Christ Jesus thought of himself.
He had equal status with God but didn't think so much of
himself that he had to cling to the advantages of that status
no matter what. Not at all. When the time came, he set
aside the privileges of deity and took on the status of a slave,
became human! Having become human, he stayed human.
It was an incredibly humbling process. He didn't claim
special privileges. Instead, he lived a selfless, obedient life
and then died a selfless, obedient death—and the worst
kind of death at that—a crucifixion.*
PHILIPPIANS 2:5–8 MSG

*Because of that obedience, God lifted him high and
honored him far beyond anyone or anything, ever,
so that all created beings in heaven and on earth—
even those long ago dead and buried—will bow in worship
before this Jesus Christ, and call out in praise that he is
the Master of all, to the glorious honor of God the Father.*
PHILIPPIANS 2:9–11 MSG

Knowing God as Adonai

To know the Lord as Adonai is both to bow before Him in absolute surrender *and* to live for Him in grateful dependence and
love. It is saying:

> *My King, I bow before You in worship.
> My Lord, You own all of me and everything about me.
> My Master, I serve, when, how, and who You want,
>   no matter what.
> My God, I trust You to meet my needs.*

BIG THOUGHT:

**Adonai is our Lord and Master.
He must be obeyed and trusted.**

Quote to Ponder

Now, as long as a man submits to the Lordship of Jesus Christ, he can count on Christ to protect him and provide for him.
LEHMAN STRAUSS[3]

Questions to Consider

1. What caught your attention as you read this chapter on Adonai?
2. Do you believe you could label yourself as a bondservant of Jesus Christ? Explain your answer.

KNOWING GOD BY HIS ATTRIBUTES: THE GREATNESS OF GOD

God Is Great

How many times in the last month have you felt or said any of the following?

- I am too busy.
- I am tired.
- I didn't know that.
- I was wrong about that.
- I can only be at one place at a time.
- I am overwhelmed.
- I don't understand.
- I am running out of time.
- I don't have enough.
- I don't know.
- I need some help.
- I can't do that.
- I am not perfect.

God has never felt or said any of those things. He is not bound by time. There is nothing that God does not know. He is righteous and perfect. He exists in all places at the same time. He has unlimited strength, energy, and power. He possesses all discernment.

God is eternal. He always has more than enough. He knows absolutely everything about everything. God always has been and always will be. He has never needed—nor will He ever need—anything. He can do anything. He does not change.

God is the only infinite being or thing in the universe. He is the greatest being of all.

God Is Infinite

When we say that God is infinite, we are saying that He has no limitations. He is bound only by His own choices. Theologian Augustus Strong summarized it well when he said, "God is unlimited, unbounded, unconfined, unsearchable, immeasurable, beyond ultimate comprehension."[1] Paul wrote,

> *Oh, the depth of the riches of the wisdom and knowledge of God! How unsearchable his judgments, and his paths beyond tracing out!*
> Romans 11:33

Humans are finite. All we have ever known is a life of limitation—in terms of time, space, strength, and knowledge. Therefore, the vastness that is God is beyond our ability to comprehend. A. W. Tozer wrote,

> *Of all that can be thought and said about God, His infinitude is the most difficult to grasp. Even to try to conceive of it would appear to be self-contradictory, for such conceptualization requires us to undertake something which we know at the outset we can never accomplish. Yet we must try, for the Holy Scriptures teach that God is infinite and, if we accept His other attributes, we must of necessity accept this one too.[2]*

God is unlimited in terms of time

God is eternal, absolutely free from the tyranny of time. Time measures something from its beginning point, but God has no beginning or end. He perpetually dwells *beyond* the realm of time. God lives in a never-ending present. It is not that He was or that He will be, but that He *is*, always and forever, I AM (Exodus 3:13–14). We will discuss the eternal nature of God in more detail on Day 17.

GOD IS UNLIMITED IN TERMS OF SPACE

God is present everywhere at once. This is called *omnipresence* (see 1 Kings 8:27; Jeremiah 23:24). Again, Dr. Strong helps us to understand when he writes, "God, in totality of His essence, without diffusion, or expansion, multiplication, or division, penetrates and fills the universe in all of its parts."[3] We will discuss God's presence in more detail on Day 18.

GOD IS UNLIMITED IN TERMS OF KNOWLEDGE

God possesses knowledge of all things—completely, perfectly, simultaneously, and innately. This is called *omniscience* (see Psalm 147:5; Isaiah 40:13-14; Romans 11:33).

GOD IS UNLIMITED IN TERMS OF POWER

God can do anything that does not contradict His own nature or will. This is called the *omnipotence* of God (see Psalm 147:5; Isaiah 40:28; Jeremiah 32:17; Revelation 19:6). We will discuss God's power in more detail on Day 16.

GOD IS UNLIMITED IN ALL HIS ATTRIBUTES

Infinity permeates every attribute of God. What God is, He is without limit. Therefore, there is no limit to His power, knowledge, perfection, love, grace, wisdom, righteousness, or kindness. A. W. Tozer writes, "In Him all of His attributes are one. All of God does all that God does; He does not divide Himself to perform a work but works in the totality of His being."[4]

GOD IS SELF-EXISTENT AND SELF-SUFFICIENT

God is *self-existent* (Exodus 3:14). The I AM has always been exactly all that He is. He has underived existence. He never came into being. He has always been. He is the cause of all, but He was caused by none.

There was a time when I could not say "I am," because I was not yet even conceived. But there was never a time when God could not say "I am," because He always was. God is the only being or thing in the universe that is self-existent.

God is also *self-sufficient* (Psalm 50:10–12). He is the only being or thing that has never in the past, does not in the present, and will not in the future have any need that is not fully met in His own being. God exists because He exists. He is not dependent on anyone for anything. He is not accountable or responsible to anyone else. Our relationship with Him is purely a gift to us on His part.

Simply speaking, God does not need us. But our very existence is dependent upon Him—and is only enhanced by our relating to Him. As a sunbeam has no existence apart from the sun, man has no existence apart from God. Any person who thinks God needs him or her is deluded. People who think they do not need God are deceived.

God is a fact. God is He whether anyone believes in Him or not. Our belief or lack of belief does not make God any more or less real. Even if everyone became an atheist, that would change absolutely nothing about God.

By the way, the very thought of atheism is ridiculous. As David observed, "The fool says in his heart, 'There is no God'" (Psalm 14:1).

GOD DOES NOT CHANGE

God is *immutable*, which means that He does not change (Hebrews 1:10–12; 13:8; James 1:17). He may on occasion alter His dealings with humanity, but His character and nature do not change.

There are no degrees in God. He is all that He is without growth or decline, addition or subtraction, development or digression. He has not aged, gotten tired, grown weaker, or become senile. God has not mutated. He has not developed a bad temper. He has not put on weight.

God does not change. All that He is, He has always been. All that He has been, He always will be.

This immutability is a great comfort, because the mighty God who had the genius and power to create the universe still has infinite genius and power. The God who loves us enough to send His Son to bring us eternal life still loves us enough to give us eternal life. The God who was willing and able to answer our prayer years ago is still the same God.

Knowing God as Great

So when we come to understand the greatness of God, what does it mean to us? How should this realization and knowledge change the way we live?

WE SHOULD WORSHIP HIM ALONE

No one and nothing else has been, is now, or ever will be what God was, is, and always will be. He alone is infinite, eternal, omnipotent, omniscient, and omnipresent. He alone is self-existent, self-sufficient, and immutable. He alone is God.

The God-shaped void that our Creator placed in every human heart cannot be adequately filled by anything other than Himself. Everything else, when placed in the spot reserved for the infinite, unlimited God, will prove to be limited, inadequate, and ultimately unfulfilling.

The Bible lists over thirty false gods by name. But in actuality, anything we devote ourselves to will prove to be an inadequate god. Even very good things—families, spouses, children, jobs, careers, health, positive hobbies—cannot take the place of the true and infinite God. All are limited, and therefore, inadequate.

Throughout the scriptures, God is adamant that there are no other gods besides Himself:

> "I am the LORD, and there is no other; there is no God besides Me. . . . I am the LORD, and there is no other."
> ISAIAH 45:5–6 NKJV

> To you it was shown, that you might know that
> the LORD Himself is God; there is none other besides Him. . . .
> Therefore know this day, and consider it in your heart, that
> the LORD Himself is God in heaven above and on the earth
> beneath; there is no other.
> DEUTERONOMY 4:35, 39 NKJV

"You are My witnesses. Is there a God besides Me?
Indeed, there is no other Rock; I know not one."
ISAIAH 44:8 NKJV

WE SHOULD TRUST HIM

Finite, false gods will not be able to help us. Only an infinite God can.

> *"When you cry out, let your collection of idols deliver you.*
> *But the wind will carry them all away, a breath will*
> *take them. But he who puts his trust in Me shall possess*
> *the land, and shall inherit My holy mountain."*
> ISAIAH 57:13 NKJV

The Lord reminds us of God's eternality, His infinite strength, and His unlimited understanding as good reasons to trust Him:

> *"Do you not know? Have you not heard? The LORD is the*
> *everlasting God, the Creator of the ends of the earth.*
> *He will not grow tired or weary, and his understanding*
> *no one can fathom. He gives strength to the weary and*
> *increases the power of the weak. Even youths grow tired*
> *and weary, and young men stumble and fall; but those*
> *who hope in the LORD will renew their strength. They*
> *will soar on wings like eagles; they will run and not*
> *grow weary, they will walk and not be faint."*
> ISAIAH 40:28–31

In one sense, every chapter of this book leads us to the same place: a deeper trust in God. From a variety of angles and perspectives, the evidence all points to this—that the infinite God is trustworthy, so trust Him. (We will discuss this further on Day 22.)

God is eternal. Therefore, trust His timing.

God is present. Therefore, trust that He is with you right now.

God knows all things. Therefore, trust His plan, even when you don't understand.

God is almighty. Therefore, trust that He can do everything

He promises and plans.

God needs no one, but He can work through anyone. Therefore, trust Him to use you to make a difference for someone each day.

BIG THOUGHT:

God is infinite, self-existent, and immutable. We should worship Him alone and trust Him completely.

Quotes to Ponder

Worship rises and falls on our concept of God. . . . And if there is one terrible disease in the Church of Christ, it is we do not see God as great as He is.
A. W. Tozer[5]

Never be afraid to trust an unknown future to a known God.
Corrie ten Boom[6]

Questions to Consider

1. What aspect of God's greatness—His eternality, omnipotence, omnipresence, omniscience, or immutability—caught your attention? Why?
2. Which is easier for you, worshipping God or trusting Him?

KNOWING GOD BY HIS ATTRIBUTES:
THE GREATNESS OF GOD

God Is Big Enough

Without exception, all Christians will at some point find themselves in a situation that is too big, too hard, too painful, or too complicated for them to handle. At that point, the question is not, "How big am I?" No—the question is, "How big is God?"

The answer is, *"Big enough!"* He is more than able to address your situation, right now.

God Is Large Enough

Some problems tower over us. We cower below them in fear. But God dwarfs every problem we face. Remember, He is infinite and omnipresent. He fills the universe in all of its parts.

When King Solomon considered the temple he had built in Jerusalem, he said, "Will God indeed dwell on the earth? Behold, heaven and the highest heaven cannot contain You, how much less this house which I have built!" (1 Kings 8:27 NASB). Or, as the prophet Jeremiah put it, "'Can a man hide himself in hiding places so I do not see him?' declares the LORD. 'Do I not fill the heavens and the earth?' declares the LORD" (Jeremiah 23:24 NASB).

God is bigger than your problem.

God Is Smart Enough

Some problems perplex us. But nothing you face is too complicated for God to figure out. Nothing confuses or confounds Him. Remember, He is omniscient. He alone has unlimited knowledge of all things past, present, and future—whether actual or possible. He knows all that can be known of everything that has existed, currently exists, will exist, or could exist.

Being *eternal*, God is already in the future. He sees what to us has yet to come—but to Him occurs in present time. God fully understands everything that has ever happened, is happening, or will happen. Being *omnipresent*, He is witness to everything everywhere. He sees everything (Hebrews 4:13; Proverbs 15:3). Being *omniscient*, He understands every bit of information with perfect understanding.

> *Great is our Lord. . . . His understanding is infinite.*
> PSALM 147:5 NASB

> *Who can fathom the Spirit of the LORD, or instruct the LORD as his counselor? Whom did the LORD consult to enlighten him, and who taught him the right way? Who was it that taught him knowledge, or showed him the path of understanding?*
> ISAIAH 40:13–14

> *Oh, the depth of the riches and wisdom and knowledge of God! How unsearchable are His judgments and decisions and how unfathomable and untraceable are His ways!*
> ROMANS 11:33 AMP

God knows our thoughts (Psalm 44:21; 139:2), our words (Psalm 139:4), and our deeds (Psalm 139:2; Revelation 2:19). God knows our sorrows (Exodus 3:7), our needs (Matthew 6:32), and our limitations (Psalm 103:14).

God knows what you are going through and what to do about it.

God Is Strong Enough

Some problems overwhelm us. They wear us down and wear us out. Some problems overpower us. They pound us into submission.

But God is not overpowered by anything. His strength, power, energy, and authority are unlimited. He is omnipotent. He is the Almighty God.

Great is our Lord and abundant in strength.
PSALM 147:5 NASB

*Do you not know? Have you not heard? The Everlasting God,
the LORD, the Creator of the ends of the earth does not
become weary or tired. His understanding is inscrutable.*
ISAIAH 40:28 NASB

*"Ah, Sovereign LORD, you have made the heavens and
the earth by your great power and outstretched arm.
Nothing is too hard for you."*
JEREMIAH 32:17

*Then I heard something like the voice of a great multitude
and like the sound of many waters and like the sound
of mighty peals of thunder, saying, "Hallelujah!
For the Lord our God, the Almighty, reigns."*
REVELATION 19:6 NASB

As Creator, God has infinite power over nature (Genesis 1). He measures the seas in His hand (Isaiah 40:12). He sees the islands as specks of dirt (Isaiah 40:15). He is almighty, with authority over all the affairs of men and nations (Daniel 4:17, 30–32). He has power over death (Hebrews 2:14,15; Revelation 1:18).

God Is More Than Enough

God is big enough to exist outside the realm of our human comprehension. He is big enough to be far beyond us in quality of being.

God is a spirit—to Him, magnitude and distance have no meaning. So when I say that God is above and beyond us, I'm not talking in terms of distance but of essence. God has a completely different kind of existence than we do. This is what theologians describe as His *transcendence*. He is not merely a few notches above us, He is infinitely beyond us—to the extent of being something entirely other than us (or anything else He created).

There are only two basic kinds of existence: God's, and that of everything else He created. While humans are like God in some ways, there are also qualities that only He possesses:

- God is infinite.
- God is eternal, with no beginning or end.
- God has unlimited strength and knowledge.
- God is unbound by space or time.
- God has no needs—He is self-sufficient.
- God is unchanging.
- God is perfect.
- God is sovereign over all, and above all.

It is not that God has just enough knowledge and strength to help us. God has infinitely more than enough. The problems that seem so impossibly large to us are tiny to Him. He is more than enough.

God Is Big Enough!

Many Bible characters faced problems as bad as, if not worse than, the ones we face today. And they all found that God was big enough to see them through.

"IS ANYTHING TOO HARD FOR THE LORD?"

Abraham was ninety-nine years old and Sarah was ninety. The Bible states that they were biologically incapable of having a child, because the reproductive aspects of their bodies were "dead." But God had promised them an heir, a son who would become the father of a nation.

Abraham and Sarah were skeptical. They looked at themselves and saw that they were insufficient. It was impossible. Sarah even laughed at the notion.

Then God asked them, "Is anything too hard for the LORD?" (Genesis 18:14).

The answer came nine months later when Sarah delivered a healthy baby boy. The Lord proved that nothing—even causing a ninety-year-old woman to have a baby—was too hard for Him!

The question is not, "Are we big enough?" The question is,

"How big is God?"

The answer: "Big enough! Nothing is too hard for God."

"GOD CAN DO ALL THINGS"

Job faced an overwhelming number of huge problems (Job 1–2). They caused Job to cry out to God for at least an audience, if not an explanation. When God showed up to give Job a tour of some hidden aspects of creation, Job humbly replied, "I know that you can do all things; no purpose of yours can be thwarted" (Job 42:2).

The question is never, "What can *we* do?" Because the answer to that question is, "Not enough."

The question is, "What can *God* do?" And the answer is, "All things. God is big enough!"

"NOTHING IS TOO HARD FOR THE LORD"

Babylon had Jerusalem under siege. Jeremiah had been shut up in jail by Zedekiah, king of Judah, who disliked the prophetic warning he'd given. Jeremiah prayed, "Ah, Sovereign LORD, you have made the heavens and the earth by your great power and outstretched arm. Nothing is too hard for you" (Jeremiah 32:17). God replied, "Behold, I am the LORD, the God of all flesh. Is there anything too hard for Me?" (Jeremiah 32:27 NKJV).

"WITH GOD NOTHING WILL BE IMPOSSIBLE"

One day, the angel Gabriel appeared to a girl named Mary, telling her that she was to bear a son, the Messiah. Since she was a virgin, this announcement shocked and perplexed her. But the angel told her to believe, "For with God nothing will be impossible" (Luke 1:37 NKJV).

The issue was not, "Is a virgin able to have a baby?" (The logical answer to that question is "no.") The question is, "Is God big enough to cause a virgin to bear a child?"

That answer came soon afterward, as Mary realized she was pregnant.

How big is God?

Big enough.

Nothing is too big, too hard, too complex, too much for God. Nothing is impossible with Him.

Knowing God as Big Enough

If we know God is big enough, we should trust Him. Living a life of faith is simple, but not easy. It is simple in that we only have to trust God. It is difficult because we can see the problems in front of us, but we can't see Him. So we must view adverse circumstances through the eyes of faith rather than sight, through the lens of trust rather than sense. As author Jerry Bridges puts it, "We must learn to trust when we don't understand."[1]

GOD IS BIG ENOUGH—THEREFORE, FOCUS ON HIM AND NOT THE PROBLEM

One time, Jesus' disciples were in a boat on the Sea of Galilee in the middle of the night—but Jesus was not with them. When a huge storm blew up, Jesus unexpectedly came to the disciples, *walking on the water* (Matthew 14:25). Peter felt compelled to join Jesus, and Jesus invited him to step out of the boat.

As long as Peter kept his eyes fixed on Jesus, he was able to walk on the water too (Matthew 14:29). But the moment he focused on the size of the waves and the strength of the wind, Peter began to sink (Matthew 14:30).

So it is with us. We will face immense and terrifying storms. If we look at the size of the tempest, we will be sunk. But when we keep our eyes on the size of our infinite God, our faith will hold.

GOD IS BIG ENOUGH—THEREFORE, TRUST THAT HE IS WORKING THROUGH YOUR PROBLEM

The apostle Paul experienced more than his share of suffering and sorrow. After becoming a Christian, he was initially rejected by church leaders. He experienced a massive amount of persecution by both pagans and Jews. He was distrusted by many, and false teachers in Corinth attempted to discredit him. Plus, he was robbed, beaten, shipwrecked, jailed, and stoned.

At the end of his life, Paul was forsaken by some of his

companions and colleagues. Yet he maintained a positive perspective, because he believed God was big enough to take all of his experiences and turn them into good.

> And we know that in all things God works for the good of those who love him, who have been called according to his purpose.
> ROMANS 8:28

Like Paul, we need to know that God is big enough to use even the worst things that happen to us to accomplish good.

BIG THOUGHT:

God is big enough (large enough, smart enough, strong enough, more than enough) to handle anything you face. Trust Him.

Quote to Ponder

> *Worry implies that we don't quite trust that God is big enough, powerful enough, or loving enough to take care of what is happening in our lives.*
> FRANCIS CHAN[2]

Questions to Consider

1. When has God proven Himself big enough in your past?
2. What aspect of God's being "big enough" appeals to you right now? Why?

KNOWING GOD BY HIS ATTRIBUTES:
THE GREATNESS OF GOD

God Is Eternal

"Do you know the time?" I innocently asked an old man seated by himself at the coffee shop.

"Time?" The man spat the word out. "Son, time is a thief. I once was young and energetic. I could go and do, and go some more. But time has robbed me of my youth, my strength, my optimism. Time robbed me of my parents, my brother, and my wife."

I nodded, not quite sure what to say or do.

"Time is relentless," he continued, shaking his finger back and forth. "The clock keeps ticking, and there is nothing you or I can do to slow it down."

His milky brown eyes bore into me as his lip curled over his front teeth. "I hate time."

Humans have issues with time. When we are young, there is never enough of it. As we get old, it passes too quickly. Regarding time, something never feels quite right. Solomon told us that's because God has etched eternity into our hearts.

He has made everything beautiful and appropriate in its time. He has also planted eternity [a sense of divine purpose] in the human heart [a mysterious longing which nothing under the sun can satisfy, except God]— yet man cannot find out (comprehend, grasp) what God has done (His overall plan) from the beginning to the end.
ECCLESIASTES 3:11 AMP

God Is Eternal

God is infinite in existence. He is absolutely free from the tyranny of time. He is eternal.

Time measures things from a beginning point, but God has no beginning or end. He perpetually dwells beyond the realm of time. He lives in a never-ending present. The issue is not what He was or will be, but that He is always and forever, *I AM* (Exodus 3:14).

> *The eternal God is your refuge, and underneath*
> *are the everlasting arms.*
> DEUTERONOMY 33:27

> *You, O LORD, shall endure forever, and the*
> *remembrance of Your name to all generations.*
> PSALM 102:12 NKJV

> *"I am the Alpha and the Omega," says the Lord God,*
> *"who is, and who was, and who is to come, the Almighty."*
> REVELATION 1:8

God Started It All

"Where did God come from?" It's a question we ask as children, grappling with the immensity that is God. But God had no origin. He did not come into being because He has always been. He will never go out of being because He always will be. God is the eternal I AM (Exodus 3:14).

"Who made God?" is another one of our childlike questions. But no one made God. God is the uncaused cause of all.

"In the beginning, God. . ." (Genesis 1:1). The first four words of the Bible declare that God was the first thing. He perpetually remains the unconditional priority of His universe. God Himself states, "I am the Alpha and the Omega" (Revelation 1:8). By this He makes Himself to be both the beginning *and* end of all things. But He Himself had no beginning and He will have no end because He is self-existent and eternal.

God Dwells Beyond Time

When we say that God is eternal, we mean that He dwells beyond the scope of space and time. To explain this, the noted Christian thinker and author C. S. Lewis suggested that we imagine a sheet of paper infinitely extended in all directions. That would represent eternity. On that paper, draw a short line to represent time. The line would have a point where it begins, and also when it ends. As the line begins and ends in that infinite expanse of paper, so time began and will end in God.[1]

Author A. W. Tozer wrote,

> Time marks the beginning of created existence, and because God never began to exist it can have no application to Him. . . . He has no past and no future. . . . God dwells in eternity but time dwells in God. He has already lived all our tomorrows as He has lived all our yesterdays.[2]

It stretches the mind to realize that God is capable of seeing the past, present, and future all at once. Let me illustrate.

Picture a parade marching down a street: there is a series of floats, a couple of high school marching bands, a few inflatable balloon characters, a group of clowns, and some classic cars. Next to the street is a high wooden fence with a knothole.

Imagine standing on tiptoes, watching the parade through the hole. You only see what is right in front of your eyes. Your perspective is limited.

Now picture God, high above the parade. He can see the beginning, the middle, and the end, all at once.

When it comes to time, our perspective is very limited. We only see what is right in front of us—our immediate present. But God is beyond the boundaries of time—He sees it all. In fact, everything that *will* happen has *already happened* from God's perspective.

The Eternal God Is Very Patient

The Old Testament repeatedly refers to God as compassionate and gracious, "slow to anger" and abounding in love and faithfulness (Exodus 34:6; Numbers 14:18; Psalm 86:15; Joel 2:13). This combination of patience and mercy explains why we have not been consumed by His wrath against sin.

Toward the end of his last letter, the apostle Peter speaks of scoffers who will mock those of us who eagerly await the return of Jesus (2 Peter 3). Then he explains the supposed slowness of Christ's return in light of the eternal patience of God.

> But do not forget this one thing, dear friends: With the Lord a day is like a thousand years, and a thousand years are like a day. The Lord is not slow in keeping his promise, as some understand slowness. Instead he is patient with you, not wanting anyone to perish, but everyone to come to repentance.
> 2 PETER 3:8–9

Why has it taken nearly two thousand years for Jesus to return to earth in glorious victory? Because God sees time differently than we do. For the One who dwells outside time, "a day is like a thousand years, and a thousand years are like a day." Therefore, He is willing to be very patient—literally, to "suffer a long time"—because every day that Jesus delays His return more people can be saved. "Bear in mind that our Lord's patience means salvation," Peter wrote (2 Peter 3:15). Where would we be if He returned the day *before* we were to be saved?

The Eternal God Is Our Safe Shelter

Moses is understood as the author of two psalms—90 and 91. In them he described God's eternality as a secure place of protection and provision for all generations.

> Lord, you have been our dwelling place throughout all generations. Before the mountains were born or you brought forth the whole world, from everlasting to everlasting you are God.
> PSALM 90:1–2

*A thousand years in your sight are like a day that
has just gone by, or like a watch in the night.*
PSALM 90:4

*Whoever dwells in the shelter of the Most High will rest in
the shadow of the Almighty. I will say of the LORD, "He is
my refuge and my fortress, my God, in whom I trust."*
PSALM 91:1-2

Moses also spoke of the brevity and mortality of humanity.

*You turn people back to dust, saying, "Return to dust, you
mortals."... Yet you sweep people away in the sleep of death—
they are like the new grass of the morning: In the morning it
springs up new, but by evening it is dry and withered.*
PSALM 90:3, 5-6

*Our days may come to seventy years, or eighty, if our strength
endures; yet the best of them are but trouble and sorrow,
for they quickly pass, and we fly away.*
PSALM 90:10

This combination—the eternality of God and the brevity of man—
led Moses to offer a simple prayer: "Teach us to number our days,
that we may gain a heart of wisdom" (Psalm 90:12). In other
words, "Help us develop the wisdom we need to fully live our
temporary life on earth, one that prepares us to live an eternal
life in heaven."

Knowing God as Eternal

Only a handful of things in this world will last forever. The rest,
"will pass away" (Matthew 24:35). The Bible reveals only five in-
vestments that are eternal in nature, and wisdom tells us to invest our lives in them:

- *God* (Deuteronomy 33:27).
- *People's souls* (John 5:28-29).

- *God's Word* (Isaiah 40:8).
- *Prayers* (Revelation 5:6–8).
- *True fellowship* (Malachi 3:16).

Randy Alcorn, founder of Eternal Perspective Ministries, has spent most of his adult life calling people to develop the wisdom to live each day in view of eternity.

> *When we view today in light of the long tomorrow, the little choices become tremendously important. Whether I read my Bible today, pray, go to church, trust Christ through suffering, share my faith, and give my money—actions graciously empowered not by my flesh but by His Spirit—is of eternal consequence, not only for other souls, but for mine.*[3]

I find that living with an eternal perspective helps me to be less stressed about today's problems—because nearly all of them will be forgotten a hundred years from now. It also helps me not to waste time, energy, and effort on things that will not last. Instead, I can focus on those things that will last forever.

BIG THOUGHT:

**God is eternal. This should give us comfort
and motivate us to live today in preparation for tomorrow.**

Quote to Ponder

> *When Christians realize that their citizenship is in heaven, they begin acting as responsible citizens of earth. They invest wisely in relationships, because they know they're eternal. Their conversations, goals, and motives become pure and honest because they realize these will have a bearing on everlasting reward.*
> JONI ERICKSON TADA[4]

Questions to Consider

1. What did you find most interesting or challenging about the eternality of God?
2. What about your present lifestyle needs to be examined and changed in view of living for eternity?

18

KNOWING GOD BY HIS ATTRIBUTES:
THE GREATNESS OF GOD

God Is Present

One attribute of God that sets Him apart from everything and everyone else is His *omnipresence*. The word comes from the Latin *omni*, meaning "all," and *praesens*, meaning "present" or "at hand." So God is fully present everywhere, at every time. Lehman Strauss observes, "The manifestations of His glory may vary at different times and places, but He Himself is present at every spot of His vast creation."[1]

Hungry for God

Several years ago, I grappled with the gnawing realization that something was missing from my life. I had been a highly committed follower of Jesus, yet deep inside something felt amiss.

Twenty years earlier, I had traded being drunk with homemade wine for being madly in love with God (Ephesians 5:18). He became my joy, my anchor, my friend, my Savior, my Master, my God. I loved everything about Him. The highlight of my day was our daily, hour-long prayer time, when I would pour out my heart into His listening ears. His presence was my magnificent obsession. I relished just being with God.

Yet now I missed Him.

I understood that God often temporarily withdraws a sense of His presence to help us mature in our faith. But this was more than that. It was a long, lonely rut of desert desperation.

Too busy in the ministry and raising a family, I had begun relating to God purely from my head and will, not from a heart on

112 — Dave Earley

fire. Though I was still strong in my faith, I was appalled to catch myself going through spiritual routines, whipping out prayers by rote. I realized that the flames of my "first love" were dangerously low.

My holy hunger to know God had faded. That aching urgency to be with God had left. I knew I needed something more than merely going through the motions—I needed God Himself.

No one-time emotional experience was the answer. What I had to have was a deeper encounter with God in both my mind and my emotions—and a greater sense of God's presence in my daily life. But I wasn't sure what to do.

Then, while reading through the Bible, I noticed that some people experienced the presence of God in a special way. I called this special awareness "the Immanuel (God with Us) Factor."

You may be thinking, *But isn't God with us all the time?* The answer is yes and no. We need to distinguish the four expressions of the presence of God.

The Four Expressions of the Presence of God

1. THE OMNIPRESENCE OF GOD

The first level is the theological term we've already mentioned. *Omnipresence* means that God is everywhere present and present everywhere. He is infinite; therefore, He is fully present in all places at the same time. The omnipresence of God touches everyone and everything in the universe. He is just as fully present in outer space or the deepest ocean as He is in Jerusalem. While *we* can't be in two places at once, God can be fully present in every place at the same time.

The omnipresence of God is like air. It's always there, but we pay little attention to it—unless for some reason it is suddenly removed.

2. THE HEAVENLY PRESENCE OF GOD

We call the second level of God's presence the "heavenly presence." It only affects those who are in heaven, where God's presence is experienced in an unlimited way. God's presence is unhindered and unrestricted there—heaven is all God, all the time. We will see Him continually (Psalm 17:15), which is what makes heaven so heavenly!

Because God is light (1 John 1:5), heaven is full of light (Revelation 21:23–25; 22:5). As God is creative, excellent, loving, joyful, encouraging, faithful, true, good, and holy, so heaven is a marvelously holy place, overflowing with all that is beautiful and truly excellent, running over with love, joy, encouragement, truth, and peace. Heaven is the sphere where the heavenly presence of God is unleashed.

3. *THE ABIDING PRESENCE OF GOD*

The third level of God's presence could be called the "abiding presence," as Hebrews 13:5 (NKJV) describes: "I will never leave you nor forsake you." God's children enjoy this promise because it gives us such sweet comfort. But it is only extended to the followers of God.

This abiding presence of God is like the sun. The sun is always there, but at times clouds hide it from view. At night, its rays are not directly experienced.

Prior to meeting God through faith in Christ, our souls only know spiritual darkness. But after meeting God, our eyes are opened to the delights of spiritual light. We are glad that God's abiding presence is always with us, and we are comforted by its warmth and light. After a while though, we may begin to take it for granted.

4. *THE MANIFEST PRESENCE OF GOD*

The "manifest presence" of God is His personality made obvious, tangible, and visible in us, around us, and for us. It is like walking in the direct sunshine, yet much more. It is God's creative, excellent, living, loving, joyful, encouraging, faithful, true, good, and holy presence flowing around and within us. It is having a distinctive aura of God punctuating and permeating everything about us. It is God at work in our lives.

Immanuel: God with Us

The Greek word *Immanuel* means "God with us." God is not a distant deity. He can become a close companion and an accessible ally. His presence is not something that is only offered to someone else. It is available to each of us.

While God's presence is constant, the choices we make can affect how we experience it. We can go through life blind to God, comprehending little of Him as His omnipresence goes largely unnoticed. We who have become His children through faith in Jesus Christ are comforted by His abiding presence, and we will ultimately revel in His heavenly presence.

But between our salvation and eternity, the goal is to be aware of and experience God's manifest presence. As one man has said, "The knowledge that God is present is blessed, but to *feel* His presence is nothing less than sheer happiness."[2]

If we want to experience some measure of heaven on earth, and if we are willing to meet the conditions prescribed in the Word of God, then we can experience the *manifest* presence of God. God is available to all of us, but how much of God we experience is up to us.

Cultivating the Manifest Presence of God

In reading through the Bible, I noticed it was said of several characters, "the Lord was with him." Their lives reveal several truths for actively experiencing the presence of God in a special way. For example:

1. Joseph enjoyed the blessing of God's manifest presence because he remained faithful to God no matter what (Genesis 39:1–22).
2. Moses so valued the presence of the Lord that he refused to lead the people without it. He cultivated this manifest presence through prayer, meeting God daily in the tabernacle (Exodus 33:7–10).
3. Joshua experienced God's manifest presence by fearlessly obeying the Lord while leading the people through the Jordan River and around the walls of Jericho (Joshua 1:1–5).

4. King Saul *lost* the manifest presence of God because of his proud rebellion (1 Samuel 16:14).
5. David so revered the manifest presence of God that his first act as king was to return the ark of the covenant to Israel (2 Samuel 6:1–22).
6. King Asa learned from both positive and negative experience that the Lord is manifestly with those who are actively with Him (2 Chronicles 15:2).
7. Jehoshaphat led his nation to experience the mighty manifest presence of the Lord when they fasted, prayed, and then went to war shouting praise and worship (2 Chronicles 20).
8. Jesus promised that those who lovingly obey His commands will experience His manifest presence (John 14:21). Jesus also promised that His followers would always experience His presence when they follow His command to make disciples (Matthew 28:19–20).

What's He Doing?

When our sons were in high school, Cathy and I were privileged to have several dozen students gather in our home every Wednesday night to study the Bible. One night we discussed what it means to go through a school day with the awareness that God is *with you*. We pointed out the fact that, even though God is already everywhere, the students could mentally "take Him with you" as they walked the halls, ate in the cafeteria, and went about their extracurricular activities.

I wasn't sure if the students got it.

A few days later the wrestling team was at a large tournament. One of the wrestlers, Keith, had been at Bible study that week. As he walked onto the mat to face a difficult opponent, I noticed that he held his right arm out, bent at a funny angle. It looked like he was escorting an invisible date.

I was standing with some of the coaches and school administrators when Keith walked out with his invisible friend. One of the adults muttered, "What's he doing?"

I gulped and said, "I think he's taking God with him."

Eyes rolled.

Keith proceeded to wrestle the best match of his life. When the referee lifted his hand afterward, Keith put his arm around his invisible friend and walked off the mat with a silly grin on his face.

"Well, whatever," one of the coaches said resignedly. "I guess it works."

To Know God as Present

Like the sun, God is present whether you feel Him or see Him. He is always there. Thank Him for being with you right now.

Throughout your day, practice His presence. Choose to mentally recognize God's presence by "taking Him with you" wherever you go.

BIG THOUGHT:

God is there to be experienced.

Quote to Ponder

In Your presence is fullness of joy; at Your right hand are pleasures forevermore.
PSALM 16:11 NKJV

Questions to Consider

1. In this chapter, what about God's omnipresence encouraged you most?
2. What can you do this week to cultivate a greater awareness of God's presence in your life?

KNOWING GOD BY HIS ATTRIBUTES: THE GREATNESS OF GOD

God Is Majestic

A few years ago, I hiked to the bottom of the Grand Canyon. On the way down, I was overwhelmed by the breathtaking views of the various levels of the canyon itself.

But, as it turned out, they were to be eclipsed by what I saw that evening.

We were staying at the very base of the immense canyon. That evening, padding out of the shower house to go back to my cabin, I happened to look up. What I saw stunned me to literal jaw-dropping.

The pitch-black sky was splattered with more diamonds than I could ever hope to count. Those stars sparkled with an intensity of light greater than I had ever seen before. Over the canyon, so far from civilization, the sky blazed without the hindrance of ambient light.

The size and scope and beauty of the sky flooded my mind with words as I tried to comprehend what I was seeing. It was immense, gigantic, enormous, colossal, and massive. It was astounding, amazing, astonishing, and awe-inspiring. It was splendid, stunning, startling, staggering, and stupefying. It was truly fabulous and fantastic, gorgeous, grand, and glorious.

I felt small, yet honored and excited. I wanted everyone to experience the majesty of the night sky.

That night, I realized what David must have felt, sitting in the wilderness of Judea under the night sky, writing songs to the One who made that sky—One who is more glorious than His creation.

Lord, our Lord, how majestic is your name in all the earth!
You have set your glory in the heavens.
PSALM 8:1

When I consider your heavens, the work of your fingers,
the moon and the stars, which you have set in place,
what is mankind that you are mindful of them,
human beings that you care for them?
PSALM 8:3–4

God Is Majestic

According to the 1828 edition of Webster's dictionary, the word *majesty* comes from a Latin term, *magis*, which means "major, more, greater." Majesty speaks of "greatness of appearance; dignity; grandeur; dignity of aspect or manner; the quality or state of a person or thing which inspires awe or reverence in the beholder; applied with peculiar propriety to God and his works."[1]

The majesty of God is also rendered by Bible translators with terms such as *splendor, excellence, glory, greatness, beauty*, and *strength*. The majesty of God refers to His greatness in terms of size, strength, knowledge, authority, beauty, and character. It speaks of the greatness of His position and His person.

God Is Majestic in His Power

Israel had been in painful slavery to the Egyptians for four hundred years. Eventually, God responded to their pleas and sent Moses to set them free. God also sent plagues—an astounding series of ten miraculous events—to overwhelm and punish the Egyptians, mock their gods, and force them to free the Israelites.

Yet, after setting God's people free, Pharaoh changed his mind. The thought of being humiliated—and of losing a free labor force—must have been more than he could stomach. The Egyptian ruler roused his army and chased after God's people.

When Pharaoh trapped them at the shores of the Red Sea, God responded with a massive miracle—He literally stood the waters high into the air, parting them for His people to walk safely through on dry ground.

The Egyptians foolishly tried to pursue the Israelites through the sea. Big mistake—God clogged the chariot wheels and released the wall of water that He had been holding back. As it crashed over them, Pharaoh's troops were all drowned.

Moses responded by leading the people in a song praising the marvelous, majestic power of the Lord.

> *"Your right hand, LORD, was majestic in power. Your right hand, LORD, shattered the enemy. In the greatness of your majesty you threw down those who opposed you. . . . By the blast of your nostrils the waters piled up. The surging waters stood up like a wall; the deep waters congealed in the heart of the sea. The enemy boasted, 'I will pursue, I will overtake them. . . . But you blew with your breath, and the sea covered them. They sank like lead in the mighty waters. Who among the gods is like you, LORD? Who is like you—majestic in holiness, awesome in glory, working wonders?"*
> EXODUS 15:6–11

God Is Majestic in His Rule

David was an obscure shepherd boy when God called him to something much greater. The Lord helped him defeat the giant Goliath, become an undefeated general, and eventually be crowned the great king of Israel. Nearing the end of his reign, David raised a great offering to build a temple to the Lord. As he reflected on God's sovereign rule—over his own life and the whole earth—David crafted a song of praise gushing over the Lord's majesty.

> *"Blessed are You, LORD God of Israel, our Father, forever and ever. Yours, O LORD, is the greatness, the power and the glory, the victory and the majesty; for all that is in heaven and in earth is Yours; Yours is the kingdom, O LORD, and You are exalted as head over all. Both riches and honor come from You, and You reign over all. In Your hand is power and might; in Your hand it is to make great and to give strength to all."*
> 1 CHRONICLES 29:10–12 NKJV

Earlier in his life, David had also written of the majesty of the Lord, "Splendor and majesty are before him; strength and joy are in his dwelling place" (1 Chronicles 16:27).

When he escaped Saul by hiding in a cave, he wrote, "Be exalted above the heavens, O God; let Your glory and majesty be over all the earth" (Psalm 57:5, 11 AMP).

Others too have ascribed praise to the Lord for the majesty of His rule.

The LORD reigns, he is robed in majesty; the LORD
is robed in majesty and armed with strength;
indeed, the world is established, firm and secure.
PSALM 93:1

Praise the LORD, my soul. LORD my God, you are very great;
you are clothed with splendor and majesty.
PSALM 104:1

Be exalted [in majesty], O God, above the heavens,
and Your glory above all the earth.
PSALM 108:5 AMP

Let them praise the name of the LORD, for his name alone
is exalted; his majesty is above earth and heaven.
PSALM 148:13 ESV

Jesus Will Be Majestic in His Return

Before coming to earth, Jesus was the fullness of God's glory and majesty (John 17:5). But He laid aside His majesty for our sake (Isaiah 53:2; Philippians 2:6–7). Although Peter, James, and John were privileged to see a brief display of Jesus' majesty, He set it aside to die as a sacrifice for our sins (1 Peter 3:18). After the resurrection, Jesus reclaimed His majesty (Revelation 1). And when He returns to earth, He will come in glorious majesty.

"For the Son of Man is going to come in the glory
and majesty of His Father with His angels, and

then He will repay each one in accordance
with what he has done."
MATTHEW 16:27 AMP

"But when the Son of Man comes in His glory and
majesty and all the angels with Him, then He
will sit on the throne of His glory."
MATTHEW 25:31 AMP

So, What?

Perhaps these verses seem distant and removed from your everyday life. What practical application can we make of God's majesty?

WE NEED A RETURN TO ACKNOWLEDGING THE MAJESTY OF GOD

Throughout history, many have recognized that individuals, families, churches, and societies suffer when there is a low view of God and a high view of man. Probably no one addressed this more passionately than A. W. Tozer, who said,

> *We need to improve the quality of our Christianity, and we*
> *never will until we raise our concept of God back to that*
> *held by apostle, sage, prophet, saint, and reformer. When*
> *we put God back where He belongs, we will instinctively*
> *and automatically move up again; the whole spiral of*
> *our religious direction will be upward.*[2]

Or, more succinctly,

> *The basis of all our trouble in religious*
> *circles is that our God is too small.*[3]

WE NEED TO RESPOND TO GOD'S MAJESTY

One of the keys to David's spiritual strength was that he knew God and responded to His glory. In Psalm 145, he showed *us* how to respond to the majesty of God with deep consideration and praise.

*I will extol You, my God, O King; and I will bless Your name
forever and ever. Every day I will bless You, and I will praise
Your name forever and ever. Great is the LORD, and greatly
to be praised; and His greatness is unsearchable. . . . I will
meditate on the glorious splendor of Your majesty, and
on Your wondrous works.*
PSALM 145:1–3, 5 NKJV

David's relationship with God was more than religious—it was
personal. What is exciting is that the majesty of God can change
each of us in deep, strong, and personal ways. Like David, we can
become people whose lives are marked by powerful praise.

BIG THOUGHT:

**God is majestic.
Knowing this should drop us to our knees
and open our mouths with words of praise.**

Quote to Ponder

Happy the soul that has been awed by a view of God's majesty.
A. W. PINK[4]

Questions to Consider

1. Can you think of a time in your life when you were over-whelmed by the majesty of God?
2. How can you cultivate an appreciation for the majesty of God in your daily life?

KNOWING GOD BY HIS ATTRIBUTES:
THE GREATNESS OF GOD

God Is the Only God

Throughout history, humanity has struggled with worshipping many gods. The belief that there are many gods is called *polytheism*. The word is a combination of *poly* (many) and *theos* (god). At base level, polytheists believe there are many different gods, each capable of doing different things. Hinduism is among many polytheistic religions today. The ancient Mayans, Greeks, and Romans all were polytheists, as were the ancient Egyptians.

As we've seen, the LORD God of the Bible is infinite. He can do all things. He is enough—more than enough—for any situation. We don't need a variety of gods to cover our needs. God can handle all your needs and those of everyone else.

God Is the Only God

To the time of the Exodus, Israel had lived under the rule of polytheistic Egyptians for four hundred years. When Moses was with God on Mount Sinai for forty days receiving the Ten Commandments, the immature Israelites grew impatient. They responded by making a golden calf and worshipping it (Exodus 32).

Years later, when Moses was preparing Israel to enter the Promised land, he knew that they would be tempted to worship the many false gods of the pagan people there. He referred to the miracle of the burning bush (Exodus 3) and the many miracles of the Exodus (Exodus 4–14) to remind them the Lord is God—and He's the only God there is (Deuteronomy 4:35). Moses' message: God is the only true God, so worship Him.

Acknowledge and take to heart this day that the LORD is God in heaven above and on the earth below. There is no other.
DEUTERONOMY 4:39

One of Moses' last official acts was to write a song of worship. The song detailed all that God had done for Israel in rescuing them from Egypt, taking them through the Red Sea, defeating their enemies, and miraculously providing for them (Deuteronomy 32). As a result, the Lord said to them, "See now that I alone am he; there is no God but me" (Deuteronomy 32:39 CSB).

There Is No Other God

After years of running from crazy King Saul and his army, David's loyalty to the true God—in spite of the awful difficulties and injustice he endured—was finally rewarded. He was rescued from the situation, and he penned a wonderful song of praise (Psalm 18). In it, David asked, "For who is God, except the LORD? And who is a rock, except our God? (Psalm 18:31 NKJV).

When he began to raise funds to build a temple for the Lord in Jerusalem, David was moved by gratitude. The Lord responded by blessing David. Out of even greater gratitude, David prayed, "This is why you are great, Lord GOD. There is no one like you, and there is no God besides you, as all we have heard confirms" (2 Samuel 7:22 CSB).

When David's son Solomon was dedicating the completed temple, he asked God for the blessing of His presence in order that "all the peoples of the earth may know that the LORD is God; there is no other" (1 Kings 8:60 NKJV).

Naaman, commander of the king of Aram's army, had leprosy. The prophet Elisha told him that the only way to be healed was to humble himself and wash seven times in the Jordan River. After initially resisting, Naaman did as he was told. God completely healed him, and Naaman became a worshipper, stating, "Indeed, now I know that there is no God in all the earth, except in Israel" (2 Kings 5:15 NKJV).

Israel's King Hezekiah faced a crushing defeat at the hands of the blasphemous Assyrian king Sennacherib and his terrifying, seemingly invincible, army. Hezekiah cried out to the Lord, "Now therefore, O Lord our God, I pray, save us from his hand, that all the kingdoms of the earth may know that You are the Lord God, You alone" (2 Kings 19:19 NKJV). The Lord sent out an angel who killed 185,000 Assyrians, which caused the others to turn tail and return home. There Sennacherib was killed by his sons (2 Kings 19:35–37).

And the prophet Isaiah recorded a series of messages from the Lord, with the exclusivity of the true God as a recurring theme:

> "Before Me there was no God formed, nor shall there be after Me. I, even I, am the Lord, and besides Me there is no savior."
> ISAIAH 43:10–11 NKJV

> "I am the First and I am the Last; besides Me there is no God."
> ISAIAH 44:6 NKJV

> "Do not fear, nor be afraid; have I not told you from that time, and declared it? You are My witnesses. Is there a God besides Me? Indeed there is no other Rock; I know not one."
> ISAIAH 44:8 NKJV

> "There is no other God besides Me, a just God and a Savior; there is none besides Me."
> ISAIAH 45:21 NKJV

> "I am God, and there is no other; I am God, and there is none like Me."
> ISAIAH 46:9 NKJV

I could continue giving examples—twenty-eight times the Bible declares that God is the only God, and there is no other God. Here are a few questions to drive the point home:

- Who other than YHWH could have possibly created us and redeemed us? No one.

- Who else is almighty, eternal, infinite, and all-knowing? No one.
- Who else is self-existent, completely self-sufficient, and absolutely sovereign? No one.
- What other deity is perfect in all of his ways? No one.
- Who else is completely good, wise, loving, merciful, just, gracious, and true? No one.
- Who else is triumphantly trustworthy? No one.

Only YHWH, the LORD, is God. There is no other.

On Your Face before the True God

At a low point in Israel's history, the people allowed the Philistines to steal their most valuable tangible treasure—the ark of the covenant. The value of the ark was not what was inside, but in who presided over it—the Lord Himself. It was designed to be a symbol of the presence of God in the midst of His people.

To the Philistines, the ark was merely a spoil of victory, just another god for them to add to their collection.

Big mistake.

The Philistines placed the ark next to a statue of their primary god, Dagon.

But the true God is not just one of many gods. He is the sovereign King of the universe before whom all others must bow. The next morning, when the Philistines entered their temple, they found Dagon flat on "his" face before the ark of the true God (1 Samuel 5:1–3)!

They tipped Dagon back up and put him back in his spot.

But the next morning, the Philistines found Dagon down again, flat on his face before the true God! This time Dagon's head and arms were broken off and were strewn across the entrance to the temple (1 Samuel 5:4–5)!

On top of that, the true God terrified the people of the town with painful tumors. They declared that their god Dagon was no match for the true God, and they sent the ark out of town as quickly as possible (1 Samuel 5:6–8).

"You Shall Have No Other Gods before Me"

The first of the top ten commands of the six hundred or so of the Old Testament is "You shall have no other gods before Me" (Exodus 20:3). This command is reiterated nineteen more times in the Bible.

Why?

Because the LORD is God. There is no other. Any other "god" is nothing but a poor substitute.

God told His people that they were not to pray to or even talk about false gods (Exodus 23:13). They were to make no covenants with false gods (Exodus 23:32). They were not to pursue, worship, serve, reverence, or sacrifice to any false gods (Deuteronomy 8:19; 2 Kings 17:35, 37). Fascination with false gods is a snare that never goes well for the people of God (Deuteronomy 7:16; 12:30).

The true God has no tolerance for false ones. When it comes to idols, God's people are to "destroy their altars, break their sacred pillars, and cut down their wooden images" (Exodus 34:13 NKJV). Why? Because God is "a jealous God" (Exodus 34:13–14; 20:5; Deuteronomy 4:23–24; 5:9; 6:15; Joshua 24:19). Knowing that He is the only true God, He is "jealous" to receive all our worship and our full, undivided devotion.

The Lord loves us. Love always seeks the highest good of its object of love. Therefore, God wants us to worship Him and Him alone because that is the absolute best for *us*.

To Know the Lord as the One and Only

We may have never bowed before a statue, but we've all been guilty of worshipping false gods. Realize that anything you worship other than the true God becomes an idol. It must be put away.

Let me ask you:

- What are your idols?
- Have you ever devoted undue time to seeking pleasure, popularity, prosperity, or prestige?

- Have you bowed before the altar of status, success, security, sports, or sex?
- Have you gone after money or material things as though they could satisfy?
- Has your religion or your ministry come ahead of your relationship with the true God?
- Have you put a relationship, a child, or your spouse ahead of God?
- Has an addiction—alcohol, drugs, gambling, sex, food, or even exercise—become your god?
- Is the false god of "self" central in your life?

I call you to put aside your idols. Install the true God as the only One in your heart.

BIG THOUGHT:

There is only one, true God.
Worship Him alone.

Quote to Ponder

No worship is wholly pleasing to God until there is nothing in me displeasing to God. . . . If there is to be true and blessed worship, some things in your life must be destroyed.
A. W. Tozer[1]

Questions to Consider

1. What are your idols?
2. What can you do to throw them down?

KNOWING GOD BY HIS ATTRIBUTES:
THE GREATNESS OF GOD

God Is Sovereign

I recently had lunch with a friend whose last few years could be described as bizarre and bad. The story includes an inexplicable firing from his job, a serious house fire, a violent crime against a family member, physical illness, and an overall sense of displacement.

We discussed the book of Job, and my friend said, "The story of Job, along with Ruth and Esther, are such great comfort because they remind me that God sees a bigger picture, has a larger plan, and always is in ultimate control."

Then he tipped his head back and smiled. "Ah, the sovereignty of God," he said. "That is the best doctrine. When life is out of control, that is the doctrine that gets me through and keeps me going."

The Sovereignty of God

The term *sovereign* describes the supreme ruler, the absolute authority. When we say, "God is sovereign," we are saying that He is the absolute and sole ruler of the universe.

> *"Yours, LORD, is the greatness and the power and the glory and the majesty and the splendor, for everything in heaven and earth is yours. Yours, LORD, is the kingdom; you are exalted as head over all."*
> 1 CHRONICLES 29:11

God is in ultimate and complete control. He has total freedom, power, and determination to do exactly as He wills. As Bible teacher Lehman Strauss noted, "God does as He pleases, only as He pleases, always as He pleases."[1] Psalmists said, "Our God is in heaven; he does whatever pleases him" (Psalm 115:3); "The LORD does whatever pleases him, in the heavens and on the earth, in the seas and all their depths" (Psalm 135:6); and, "The LORD is the great God, the great King above all gods" (Psalm 95:3).

Though we may find it hard to believe or accept, God is also sovereign in our human suffering.

GOD IS IN CONTROL WHEN LIFE IS OUT OF CONTROL

One day, life for Job seemed well-ordered, normal, and very blessed by God. The next day it spun out of control as a series of unimaginable and excruciating events erased his wealth, property, career, businesses, employees, and reputation. The devastating day ended with the report that all ten of his children had been killed in a freak accident. If that wasn't bad enough, his own health was soon under attack. Job was covered with excruciating lesions.

In his pain, Job begged God for deliverance—or at least an explanation. He questioned God's moral right to act as He had. Day after day, Job received nothing but silence from God. . .and self-righteous condemnation from his friends.

Finally, God responded. But instead of giving Job an explanation, the Lord gave him a grand tour of creation (Job 38:1–41:34). Job responded in humble acknowledgement of God's sovereignty.

> Then Job answered the LORD: "I am unworthy—how can I reply to you? I put my hand over my mouth. I spoke once, but I have no answer—twice, but I will say no more."
> JOB 40:3–5

> Then Job replied to the LORD: "I know that you can do all things; no purpose of yours can be thwarted."
> JOB 42:1–2

Job realized that he had been wrong to question God, and he sincerely repented before his Creator King: "My ears had heard of you but now my eyes have seen you. Therefore I despise myself and repent in dust and ashes" (Job 42:5–6). Then God generously restored all Job had lost and gave him twice as much as he had before (Job 42:8–17).

This story reminds us that even when we are being cut by deep hurts or crushed by catastrophic events, we can maintain hope—because the sovereign God sees a bigger picture, has a larger plan, and always is in ultimate control. When life seems out of control, we should trust that He has it all under control.

GOD IS PURPOSEFUL WHEN WE ARE IN PAIN

David was flying high. The most popular person in the land, he had bested Goliath, gone undefeated as a general, and married the king's daughter. But King Saul soon became violently jealous and tried to kill David. He was forced to flee for his life, and spent the next several years in the wilderness hiding from Saul and his army.

Holed up in a cave, the one-time boy wonder struggled to maintain hope. But one thought kept him going: the fact that God is sovereign and purposeful even through our pain.

> I call to God Most High, to God who fulfills his purpose for me.
> PSALM 57:2 CSB

> The LORD will fulfill his purpose for me. LORD, your faithful love endures forever; do not abandon the work of your hands.
> PSALM 138:8 CSB

Therefore, even when we face an onslaught of unforeseen, undeserved, and unwanted pain, we should trust God, that He has a purpose through our pain (Romans 8:28).

Jesus Is the Sovereign King of Kings

The New Testament repeatedly uses the title "Lord Jesus Christ" (sixty times in the New Testament). Throughout Paul's letters

Jesus is referred to as "the Lord of hosts" (Romans 9:29 CSB); "Lord of all" (Romans 10:12); "Lord of both the dead and the living" (Romans 14:9); "Lord of glory" (1 Corinthians 2:8); and "Lord of peace" (2 Thessalonians 3:16). Paul finishes his first letter to Timothy with a flourish, speaking of the return of "the Lord Jesus Christ" and referring to Him as "the blessed and only Potentate, the King of kings and Lord of lords" (1 Timothy 6:15 NKJV).

Jesus' sovereign rulership was not a gift. No, He earned it at great cost through His death on the cross and resurrection from the dead. "Christ died and returned to life so that he might be the Lord of both the dead and the living" (Romans 14:9; see also Ephesians 1:19–22 and Colossians 1:13–22).

Jesus laid aside His divine attributes to become a man. Then He went beyond that to die as a sacrifice for our sins. As a result, "at the name of Jesus every knee should bow, in heaven and on earth and under the earth, and every tongue acknowledge that Jesus Christ is Lord, to the glory of God the Father" (Philippians 2:10–11). Ultimately, Jesus will defeat every enemy, exercising full dominion over the devil, demons, and every form of darkness. "Then the end will come, when he hands over the kingdom to God the Father after he has destroyed all dominion, authority and power. For he must reign until he has put all his enemies under his feet. The last enemy to be destroyed is death" (1 Corinthians 15:24–26; see also Romans 6:9, 14).

One day, Jesus will return as the Warrior King proudly displaying His title, *"King of Kings and Lord of Lords."*

I saw heaven standing open and there before me was a white horse, whose rider is called Faithful and True. With justice he judges and wages war. His eyes are like blazing fire, and on his head are many crowns. He has a name written on him that no one knows but he himself. He is dressed in a robe dipped in blood, and his name is the Word of God. The armies of heaven were following him, riding on white horses and dressed in fine linen, white and clean. Coming out of his mouth is a sharp sword with which to strike down the nations. "He will rule them with an iron scepter." He treads the winepress of the fury of

the wrath of God Almighty. On his robe and on his thigh he has this name written: KING OF KINGS AND LORD OF LORDS.
REVELATION 19:11–16

Rather than waiting until the day when everyone must bow to King Jesus, why not humbly submit our lives to Him now?

The true King of kings and Lord of lords

Nebuchadnezzar was the greatest king of the mighty Babylonian Empire. He was brutal, powerful, ambitious, and very proud. Having defeated so many other kingdoms, he thought of himself as "the king of kings" (Daniel 2:37). He even decided that he had attained the status of a god, and created a giant gold statue to himself.

Later, God strongly warned Nebuchadnezzar to humble himself—to recognize that his power, wealth, and influence were from God and not of his own making. He would have to "acknowledge that the Most High is sovereign over all kingdoms on earth and gives them to anyone he wishes" (Daniel 4:25).

Nebuchadnezzar arrogantly ignored the warning. Bad decision.

As a result, he lost everything: his throne, his wealth, his power, his pride, and even his sanity (Daniel 4:28–33). To his credit though, Nebuchadnezzar ultimately came to his senses and bowed his knee to the *true* King of kings and Lord of lords.

> *At the end of that time, I, Nebuchadnezzar, raised my eyes toward heaven, and my sanity was restored. Then I praised the Most High; I honored and glorified him who lives forever. His dominion is an eternal dominion; his kingdom endures from generation to generation. All the peoples of the earth are regarded as nothing. He does as he pleases with the powers of heaven and the peoples of the earth. No one can hold back his hand or say to him: "What have you done?"*
> DANIEL 4:34–35

Because Nebuchadnezzar humbled himself before the sovereignty of God, everything was restored to him (Daniel 4:36).

He summarized the painful lesson he learned with these words: "Now I, Nebuchadnezzar, praise and exalt and glorify the King of heaven, because everything he does is right, and all his ways are just. And those who walk in pride he is able to humble" (Daniel 4:37).

We should do what Nebuchadnezzar took too long to do—bow before the true King of kings. Let's quit trying to be the boss of our own lives and instead humble ourselves. Take your hands off the steering wheel of life, and allow the Most High God to lead.

BIG THOUGHT:

God is the sovereign ruler in ultimate control of all things. We must submit to His leadership and rest in His wisdom.

Quote to Ponder

God is in control, but in His control, He allows us to experience pain. The pain is very real. We hurt, we suffer. But in the midst of our suffering we must believe that God is in control; that He is sovereign.
JERRY BRIDGES[2]

Questions to Consider

1. How does the final quote by Jerry Bridges make you feel?
2. In what area of your life do you need to trust God to be sovereign?

KNOWING GOD BY HIS ATTRIBUTES:
THE GOODNESS OF GOD

God Is Trustworthy

At some point in life, I imagine every human being has wondered, *What is going on? Why would God allow this to happen?* For a biblical perspective, let's refer to a story in the Old Testament's book of beginnings, Genesis.

Son to Slave

Genesis tells the story of Joseph, the favored teenage son of a wealthy shepherd named Jacob. Joseph angered his ten older brothers when he told them that he'd dreamed of one day becoming their leader. They responded by taking an opportunity they had to sell Joseph to slave traders who just happened to be traveling to Egypt.

I imagine that Joseph must have wondered, "What is going on? Why did God give me the dream and then allow *this* to happen?"

Slave to Prisoner

Joseph just happened to end up serving in the house of Potiphar, Pharaoh's captain of the guard. There, Joseph performed so admirably that he was given increasing responsibilities. Here he learned about Egyptian culture and developed his leadership skills.

But it just so happened that Potiphar's wife took a fancy to Joseph. She repeatedly tried to seduce him, but to no avail. Joseph's refusal of her advances—and his loyalty to God and

Potiphar—were unjustly rewarded with evil. The woman lied about Joseph, claiming he'd tried to rape her. As a result, he was thrown in prison.

At this point, Joseph must have asked himself, "What is God doing? Why doesn't He stop this?"

In prison, Joseph again distinguished himself by his service, and was given increased responsibility. It just so happened that some of the Pharaoh's former cabinet members had also gotten themselves imprisoned. From them, Joseph probably learned about the running of Pharaoh's houseful and the inside workings of the Egyptian government.

It just so happened that one of Joseph's fellow prisoners had been Pharaoh's cupbearer. Joseph interpreted a dream the man had had, making but one request in return: that when the cupbearer was restored to his position in Pharaoh's court, he remember Joseph—who'd been unjustly enslaved and imprisoned.

But the cupbearer just happened to forget about Joseph. . . for two years.

At this point, I would guess that Joseph would have been discouraged. The situation must have felt hopeless. He was far from home, enslaved, imprisoned, forgotten, and forsaken.

Prisoner to Prime Minister

Then, it just so happened, Pharaoh had a troubling dream that none of his advisers could interpret. Finally, the cupbearer remembered Joseph and mentioned him to Pharaoh. The Egyptian ruler had Joseph brought to him and shared the details of his dream. Joseph relied on the Lord for the ability to interpret the dream, and told Pharaoh that seven years of plenty would be followed by seven years of devastating famine. Joseph then presented a plan of action to prepare for what was coming.

Pharaoh was so impressed that he made Joseph second in command, answering only to him. Wow! One day Joseph was a slave, rotting away in a dungeon prison. The next he was prime minister of Egypt!

The Senseless Now Made Sense

The nonsensical suddenly made perfect sense. The impossible became a reality.

For Joseph, God wisely brought good out of bad. The slave was liberated. The prisoner was set free. The backwoods shepherd was a top government leader. He attained a position of power that otherwise would have been impossible.

For Egypt, God wisely brought good out of bad, as she was well-prepared for a horrific famine that would otherwise have crippled her.

For the Hebrews, Joseph's people, God wisely brought good out of bad as the prime minister took care of them when the famine hit.

For over a dozen years, it had appeared that God did *not* know what He was doing. Though Joseph remained faithful to God, bad things kept happening to him.

But his bizarre and seemingly senseless journey now made perfect sense. God "just happened to know" what He was doing and orchestrated each event to create the best possible outcome.

God is smart. He knew exactly what He was doing all along.

If any of the painful pieces of this puzzle had been missing, Joseph could not have become powerful in Egypt, and he could not have saved many lives—including those of his family, who just happened to be the fledging Hebrew nation.

Every seemingly pointless and painful event had a purpose:

- Joseph had to be sold into slavery to get to Egypt.
- Joseph had to serve in Potiphar's house for the man's wife to falsely accuse him and get him thrown into prison.
- Joseph had to be in prison to meet Pharaoh's cabinet members.
- Joseph had to be forgotten two years for the timing to be right to prepare for the famine.

God Intended It for Good

Joseph understood God's hand of wisdom in his life. When his brothers came to Egypt to get food, Joseph explained to them how God's wise purpose and supervision overrode their selfish, evil act of selling him into slavery.

> *"God sent me ahead of you to preserve for you a remnant on earth and to save your lives by a great deliverance."*
> GENESIS 45:7

> *"You intended to harm me, but God intended it for good to accomplish what is now being done, the saving of many lives."*
> GENESIS 50:20

For years, Joseph's situation seemed senseless. God seemed either incapable of fixing it or unwilling to do so. But He proved to be trustworthy.

God Is Trustworthy

God is deeply committed to bringing us to a place where we must trust Him. He will repeatedly put us in seemingly hopeless situations—spots where there is no way anything good can possibly come. Why? He wants us to lose our reliance on anything and everything other than Him. God wants us to learn to trust Him in the dark, even when we cannot understand what He is doing.

GOD IS GOOD: TRUST HIM

The strong testimony of the Bible, observation, and experience is that God is good. Although we will discuss God's goodness in much more detail in Days 23–28, it is sufficient here to say this: when you add up God's love, mercy, compassion, grace, generosity, kindness, truth, justice, holiness, patience, peace, joy, and forgiveness—and you realize that they are all infinite and perfect in nature—it becomes startlingly clear that God is *very* good.

God's goodness is on every page of the Bible. If you want just a small example, leaf through the book of Psalms (25:8; 31:19;

34:8; 73:1; 86:5; 100:5; 106:1; 119:68; 145:9) to hear the drumbeat of the goodness of God.

We can trust God in our pain because God is perfectly and infinitely good.

God is smart: Trust Him

God knows everything about you and your situation. He knows what to do and He knows how to do it. He knows more than just the facts—He knows how to use those facts to accomplish a determined outcome. Robert Lightner states, "He knows how to use His unlimited knowledge to the best possible end."[1]

This means that when it comes to your suffering situation, God knows *what* you need, *when* you need it, and *how* to make it happen. He knows exactly what He is doing. You can trust God in your difficulties because He is smart.

God is powerful: Trust Him

God has absolute power, authority, strength, and energy to do anything He wants, when He wants, and exactly how He wants. Therefore, you can trust Him.

God is providential: Trust Him

When we combine God's active goodness and absolute authority over all things, we have what theologians call the "providence" of God. In the context of suffering, the apostle Paul addressed God's providence like this: "We know that in all things God works for the good of those who love him, who have been called according to his purpose" (Romans 8:28).

Jerry Bridges states, "God's providence is His constant care for and His absolute rule over all His creation for His glory and the good of His people."[2] Notice that Bridges speaks of both God's glory *and* our good resulting from the same circumstance. God sacrifices neither His glory for our good or our good for His glory. Our suffering has purpose. We can trust Him.

David declared, "The steps of a good man are ordered by the LORD" (Psalm 37:23 NKJV). In light of that truth, A. W. Tozer states that there is no such thing as an accident.

> *The man of true faith may live in the absolute assurance that*
> *his steps are ordered by the Lord. . . . To the child of God, there*
> *is no such thing as an accident. . . . Accidents may indeed ap-*
> *pear to befall him and misfortune stalk his way; but these are*
> *evils in appearance only and will seem evils only because we*
> *cannot read the secret script of God's hidden providence.*[3]

GOD IS SOVEREIGN: TRUST HIM

As we discussed on Day 21, God is sovereign. He is in absolute control of all things, great or small, including every aspect of nature, every person, every nation, and every event. What God wants done will be done, without exception. God's purposes will prevail.

> *"I know that you can do all things;*
> *no purpose of yours can be thwarted."*
> JOB 42:2

> *The plans of the LORD stand firm forever,*
> *the purposes of his heart through all generations.*
> PSALM 33:11

> *In their hearts humans plan their course,*
> *but the LORD establishes their steps.*
> PROVERBS 16:9

Knowing that God is sovereign gives us a basis to trust Him. Margaret Clarkson states, "The sovereignty of God is the one impregnable rock to which the suffering human heart must cling. The circumstances surrounding our lives are no accident. . . . God is the Lord of human history and the personal history of every member of His redeemed family."[4]

There are no accidents. God is the Lord of your personal history. Trust Him.

Trust Him

God is the most trustworthy being in the universe. Yet, when we are hurting, that can be hard to remember. The pain blinds us to the truth of God's trustworthiness.

Several years ago, I was in a confusing season of suffering. As I studied the truths about God that we have been reading about today, a simple set of encouraging truths emerged. I call them "The Trust Formula":

- God is good; therefore, He *wants* what is best.
- God is smart; therefore, He *knows* what is best and how to make it happen.
- God is almighty; therefore, He *can do* what is best.
- God is providential and sovereign, He *will do* what is best
- Therefore, I trust Him.

BIG THOUGHT:

**God is by nature trustworthy,
even when you may not feel it. Trust Him.**

Quotes to Ponder

In a universe governed by God, there are no chance events.
R. C. Sproul[5]

Questions to Consider

1. In what areas are you struggling to trust God?
2. Which aspect of the Trust Formula did you find most encouraging? Why?

KNOWING GOD BY HIS ATTRIBUTES: THE GOODNESS OF GOD

God Is Holy

I want you to picture a nation that has become commercially and militarily strong yet is rotting spiritually. See her as cancerously corrupt, riddled with the putrefying sores of sexual immorality, greedy idolatry, and religion without relationship. At the highest level, godly leadership is being replaced by untested and wicked people.

Now picture a young man who passionately loves God, one with a longing to see his nation return to God. See him broken and burdened to somehow make a difference—just like many of you.

In 739 BC, Isaiah was a restless young man in a seething nation. The last good king had died, leaving the Hebrews hanging in the balance between good and evil, God and Satan, prosperity and destruction. As a righteous and sensitive person, Isaiah felt his nation's pain, and ached to do something about it. As a God-seeker, he longed for a more intimate relationship with the Lord. God obliged both passions. Let's read how it happened.

In the year that King Uzziah died, I saw the Lord, high and exalted, seated on a throne; and the train of his robe filled the temple. Above him were seraphim, each with six wings: With two wings they covered their faces, with two they covered their feet, and with two they were flying. And they were calling to one another: "Holy, holy, holy is the LORD Almighty; the whole earth is full of his glory." At the sound of their voices the

doorposts and thresholds shook and the temple was filled with smoke. "Woe to me!" I cried. "I am ruined! For I am a man of unclean lips, and I live among a people of unclean lips, and my eyes have seen the King, the LORD Almighty." Then one of the seraphim flew to me with a live coal in his hand, which he had taken with tongs from the altar. With it he touched my mouth and said, "See, this has touched your lips; your guilt is taken away and your sin atoned for." Then I heard the voice of the Lord saying, "Whom shall I send? And who will go for us?" And I said, "Here am I. Send me!"
ISAIAH 6:1–8

"I Saw the Lord"

Isaiah was one of the few persons who'd been privileged to peer into heaven while living on earth. Can you imagine seeing the Lord? Isaiah's vision of the throne room put God in perspective: He is vastly unlike all others. God is majestic, seated on a throne. He is supreme, high and exalted. But above all, God is holy, very holy. Three powerful witnesses give testimony to God's magnificent holiness.

The first witness is the fact that God is the only being in the universe worshipped by seraphim. The Hebrew word *seraph* means "burning." We may hope that God is a big, soft teddy bear, but the Bible describes Him as a consuming fire (Hebrews 12:29). Seraphim are unique angels who fly constantly around the throne of God. Being so near to God, these asbestos-like wonders experience spontaneous and eternal combustion yet are never consumed.

The second witness to God's holiness comes from the antiphonal chants of the seraphim. They perpetually cry out, "Holy, holy, holy is the LORD Almighty; the whole earth is full of his glory" (Isaiah 6:3). God has many attributes, but those closest to Him recognize that the dominant attribute is His surpassing holiness. It is so overpoweringly pervasive that all they can do is repeat over and over, "Holy, holy, holy." It is an eternal symphony to God.

The third witness to God's holiness is Isaiah's response. When he saw God up close and personal, he did not sit down and chat, stand up and cheer, or kick back and relax. Isaiah fell down and repented. "Woe to me!" he cried. "I am ruined!" A literal translation could read, "I am condemned guilty of sin and am melting away in the oven-blast brilliancy of God's holiness."

In His mercy, God did not leave Isaiah in the misery of condemnation. Instead He saw to it that Isaiah received cleansing. Yet what especially strikes me is that God not only *cleansed* Isaiah but *called* him. Both Isaiah and God were keenly aware of Israel's need for a new prophet. In Isaiah, God had found one. Humble, clean vessels are what God wants to pour Himself through.

After Isaiah became clean, God called, "Whom shall I send? And who will go for us?" Isaiah responded, "Here am I. Send me!"

God Is Holy

The holiness of God is declared throughout the Bible. Later in the book of Isaiah, God introduces Himself by His holiness: "I am the Lord, your Holy One, Israel's Creator, your King" (Isaiah 43:15). The apostle John stated that God's holiness will be the theme of angels worshipping around His throne: "Day and night they never stop saying: 'Holy, holy, holy is the Lord God Almighty,' who was, and is, and is to come" (Revelation 4:8).

When the Bible speaks of God's holiness, it indicates that God is entirely different, utterly unique. If we think of God's holiness as simply a higher, purer version of our own goodness, we are mistaken. The fact that God is holy means that He is separate from us.

"For I am God, and not a man—the Holy One among you."
Hosea 11:9

"Who among the gods is like you, Lord? Who is like you—majestic in holiness, awesome in glory, working wonders?"
Exodus 15:11

"There is no one holy like the Lord; there is no one besides you; there is no Rock like our God."
1 Samuel 2:2

*"To whom will you compare me? Or who is
my equal?" says the Holy One.*
Isaiah 40:25

*"Who will not fear you, Lord, and bring
glory to your name? For you alone are holy."*
Revelation 15:4

God's holiness is described as that which is absolutely separate
from any and all sin. It is not that God has less sin in His nature—it
is that God has *no* sin in His nature. "Your eyes are too pure to
look on evil," the prophet Habakkuk said. "You cannot tolerate
wrongdoing" (Habakkuk 1:13).

God's holiness is intensely pure. As already mentioned, God's
holiness is of such intensity that the angels nearest Him burn
perpetually—and worship unceasingly. His holiness is so pure
that compared to us He is "a consuming fire" (Hebrews 12:29).

God's holiness is one of His primary characteristics. If we
polled most Christians and asked them for God's most important attribute, the response would probably be "love." Yes, thank
God for His love. But those angels nearest Him do not declare
His love unceasingly—they declare his *holiness*.

God's holiness is the one attribute that is declared in tripli-
cate (Isaiah 6:3; Revelation 4:8). If the Bible states something
about God once, that is enough. Two mentions should really get
our attention. But to say something three times means that it is
of utmost importance.

God's holiness is not an acquired perfection.[1] No, holiness
is an essential aspect of God's being, and has been throughout
eternity. There has never been a moment when God was not
holy. There has never been a moment when God was more or
less holy. Holiness is what God is.

Because God Is Holy. . .

When Isaiah saw the Lord and His holiness, it produced a response. As we meditate on the Lord's holiness today, it should
produce one of many possible responses in us.

CONFESS YOUR SIN

When Isaiah saw the Lord, he was quick to acknowledge his own unworthiness.

> *"Woe to me!" I cried. "I am ruined! For I am a man of unclean lips, and I live among a people of unclean lips, and my eyes have seen the King, the LORD Almighty."*
> ISAIAH 6:5

HUMBLE YOURSELF

When Isaiah saw the Lord's holiness, it crushed him. Godly humility, brokenness, and contrition are natural responses to the lofty, exalted holiness of God. Later in his prophecies, Isaiah recorded a very encouraging promise:

> *For this is what the high and exalted One says—he who lives forever, whose name is holy: "I live in a high and holy place, but also with the one who is contrite and lowly in spirit, to revive the spirit of the lowly and to revive the heart of the contrite."*
> ISAIAH 57:15

BE WILLING TO GO WHERE THE LORD SENDS AND DO WHAT THE LORD ASKS

When he saw the Lord, Isaiah not only confessed his sin but he made himself fully available. When the Lord mentioned the need for a messenger, Isaiah responded, "Here am I. Send me!" (Isaiah 6:8).

Something in the glorious holiness of God tugs at something deep within us. It calls us out of ourselves and out of our comfort zones. It compels us to go tell others that they need to repent. It beckons us to give our all in serving Him.

LIVE A CLEAN LIFE OF INTEGRITY

In Psalm 15, David paints a picture of those who gain access to God's "holy mountain" (verse 1). They live lives marked by a blameless walk, righteous actions, and truthful words (verse 2). They do not slander or slur others; they treat their neighbors right (verse 3). They despise the despicable and honor the honorable; they keep their promises no matter what (verse 4). They do not mistreat the poor (verse 5). In other words, they strive to live holy lives.

In the book of Leviticus, we see God giving His people very detailed instructions on living an externally holy life. In this context, He repeatedly calls them to be holy, since He is holy.

> "I am the LORD your God; consecrate yourselves and be holy, because I am holy. . . . I am the LORD, who brought you up out of Egypt to be your God; therefore, be holy, because I am holy."
> LEVITICUS 11:44–45; SEE ALSO 19:2; 20:7

The apostle Peter echoed this theme in his first letter when he stated, "But just as he who called you is holy, so be holy in all you do; for it is written: 'Be holy, because I am holy'" (1 Peter 1:15–16).

Now you know. Will you respond like Isaiah?

BIG THOUGHT:

God is holy.
This forces us to face our sin and embrace His love.

Quote to Ponder

> The pursuit of holiness is a joint venture between God and the Christian. No one can attain any degree of holiness without God working in his life, but just as surely no one will attain it without effort on his own part. God has made it possible for us to walk in holiness. But He has given us the responsibility of doing the walking. He does not do that for us.
> JERRY BRIDGES[2]

Questions to Consider

1. How do you feel when you consider the fact that, around the throne of God, the attribute the angels proclaim is His holiness rather than His love?

2. Which of the four suggested responses to the holiness of God resonates most with you?

KNOWING GOD BY HIS ATTRIBUTES:
THE GOODNESS OF GOD

God Is Love

It is one of the greatest love stories ever told. It's not romantic, but it is astounding, surprising, and so very encouraging. Many call it "the parable of the prodigal son."

Pharisees were criticizing Jesus because He welcomed sinners and even ate with them (Luke 15:1–2). Jesus responded by telling three parables about love for the lost. He told of the pursuit of a lost sheep (Luke 15:3–7), the finding of a lost coin (verses 8–10), and the return of a lost son (verses 11–32). In this last story, the wayward son represents each of us, anyone who has ever wandered from their father's house. The father in the parable represents God. Jesus told the story to picture the Father's amazing love for the lost—for us.

The story opens with a selfish young Jewish man demanding his inheritance while his father was still living. This was very disrespectful, but to make things worse, the young man traveled to a far country and blew through the money in wild living. That would have greatly tarnished his father's reputation.

Finally, the son realized his selfish, rebellious stupidity. Lonely, hungry, and hurting, he decided to return to his father, apologize and hope that the older man would at least allow him to work as a hired servant.

But the father responded with a surprising display of love.

"While he was still a long way off, his father saw him and was filled with compassion for him; he ran to his son, threw

his arms around him and kissed him."
LUKE 15:20

In that one verse, we see God the Father's love on grand display.

THE FATHER'S LOVE IS FORGIVING AND MERCIFUL
The custom was that if such a disrespectful son ever returned, he was to be disowned by his family and even his village. But the father did just the opposite.

THE FATHER'S LOVE IS SEEN AS PATIENT AND EXPECTANT
Even though the son had been gone for years, the father was still looking for him to return.

THE FATHER'S LOVE IS PORTRAYED AS COMPASSIONATE
When he saw his son, the father couldn't contain himself. His heart was "filled with compassion."

THE FATHER'S LOVE IS ACTIVE
The father did not wait for the young man to approach him, but instead he got up and "ran" to his son.

THE FATHER'S LOVE IS EXPRESSIVE
The father threw his arms around his son and kissed him.

These are all wonderfully encouraging truths about our Father's attitude toward us. But there is more. When the son tried to ask for forgiveness, and request a position as a hired hand, the father instead called for a celebration.

> *"The father said to his servants, 'Quick! Bring the best robe and put it on him. Put a ring on his finger and sandals on his feet. Bring the fattened calf and kill it. Let's have a feast and celebrate. For this son of mine was dead and is alive again; he was lost and is found.' So, they began to celebrate."*
> LUKE 15:22–24

THE FATHER'S LOVE IS ALSO AMAZINGLY GRACIOUS

Not only did he withhold the punishment his son deserved, the father gave the young man what he did not deserve—expensive gifts, an extravagant party in his honor, and the restoration of his position as a son in the family.

Having been a prodigal son, one who wasted years of my life on selfish, sinful living, I have felt the shame and guilt the son in this story must have felt. I know the sense of unworthiness and the feeling that I would never be granted access to the Father. I also have tasted the sweet, surprising joy of the merciful, forgiving, unexpected, undeserved, patient, active, expressive, gracious, generous, and extravagant love of God.

The Love of God

My inadequate attempt at defining God's love is this: *His voluntary, unconditional, unselfish concern for others and His sacrificial action to bring about their highest good.* In other words, God cares for you and He acts to express that compassion in the best possible way.

The Bible tells us that "God is love" (1 John 4:8). This means that God is the expression of love. But it does not mean that God is exclusively love. The rest of the Bible declares that He is much, much more—He is self-sufficient, self-existent, infinite, eternal, almighty, omniscient, sovereign, majestic, transcendent, wise, righteous, holy, and true. And that list only scratches the surface.

BECAUSE GOD IS THE EXPRESSION OF LOVE, EVERYTHING HE DOES IN EVERY MOMENT IS MARKED AND BALANCED BY LOVE

God's holiness is balanced with His love. His power is directed by His compassion. His righteous justice is coupled with His merciful grace.

GOD'S LOVE IS AN EXPRESSION AND EXTENSION OF HIS OTHER ATTRIBUTES

Because God is good, His love wants what is good for us. Because God is wise, His love knows what is best for us. Because

God is almighty, His love can do what is best for us. Because God is sovereign, His love will do what is best for us.

Because God is perfect, His love is perfect. Because God is truth, His love is real. Because God is faithful, His love is loyal. Because God is self-sufficient, His love has no beginning. Because God is eternal, His love has no end. Because God is infinite, His love has no limit. God's love is bigger than an ocean, higher than a mountain, touching us more deeply, and reaching us more completely than anything else.

GOD'S LOVE FOR US IS UNLIKE THE LOVE WE HAVE FOR ONE ANOTHER

God's love is uncaused and undeserved. God loves us because He loves us—not because we have done or will do anything to earn that love. As John wrote, "In this is love, not that we loved God, but that He loved us and sent His Son to be the propitiation for our sins" (1 John 4:10 NKJV).

God's love is undeniable. As Paul stated, "God demonstrates his own love for us in this: While we were still sinners, Christ died for us" (Romans 5:8).

God's love is sacrificial. His love gives regardless of the cost. Of course, He has already paid the ultimate price of His Son's life. "God so loved the world that he gave his one and only Son, that whoever believes in him shall not perish but have eternal life" (John 3:16). "In this the love of God was manifested toward us, that God has sent His only begotten Son into the world, that we might live through Him" (1 John 4:9 NKJV).

God's love is personal. He not only cares about people groups, He cares about individuals. He cares about the details of *your* life (Psalm 139:1–18; Matthew 10:29–31).

God's love is unstoppable.

The Invincible Love of God

The first-century church in Rome faced incredible opposition. They could lose jobs, be robbed, or suffer beatings without protection from the authorities. By the last part of the first century, to entertain the bloodthirsty masses, Romans threw Christians to wild dogs or lions to be torn apart. It was also reported that Christians were used as human torches to light Nero's gardens.

What truth could possibly strengthen people in such peril?

Paul, who was ultimately beheaded in a Roman prison, encouraged the believers by pointing to the undeniable, unstoppable, invincible, inseparable love of Christ.

> *Who shall separate us from the love of Christ? Shall*
> *trouble or hardship or persecution or famine*
> *or nakedness or danger or sword?*
> ROMANS 8:35

Paul further promised the love of Christ would not allow them to become victims—instead, they would be victors in the worst attacks imaginable. "No, in all these things we are more than conquerors through him who loved us" (Romans 8:37).

In fact, Paul concluded, there was absolutely nothing—physical, emotional, or spiritual—that could possibly separate believers from the love of Christ.

> *I am convinced that neither death nor life, neither angels*
> *nor demons, neither the present nor the future, nor any*
> *powers, neither height nor depth, nor anything else in*
> *all creation, will be able to separate us from the love*
> *of God that is in Christ Jesus our Lord.*
> ROMANS 8:38–39

Jesus Loves Me

For the last 150 years, one of the best-known songs among preschoolers has been "Jesus Loves Me." The words of the song were initially part of a long-forgotten novel, *Say and Seal*, written by sisters Anna and Susan Warner. In one scene, a grieving father attempts to comfort his dying son with the love of God, by reciting a poem:

> *Jesus loves me! This I know,*
> *For the Bible tells me so.*
> *Little ones to Him belong;*
> *They are weak, but He is strong.*[1]

Because the book was published as the American Civil War was beginning, the little poem caught the nation's interest. It was recited by scared and dying soldiers, by families whose sons and fathers had gone to war, by pastors to their people, even by the president. Put to music by noted hymn writer William Bradbury in 1862, "Jesus Loves Me" became an instant classic. In the decades since, it has simply but powerfully taught millions of people the truth of Romans 8:38–39.

The Disciple Jesus Loved

Of the twelve disciples, only one followed Jesus all the way to the foot of the cross—John. Later, he served as copastor of the thriving church of Jerusalem, and wrote an outstanding Gospel, three epistles, and the book of the Revelation! In spite of persistent heartache and fierce persecution, John went strong for Jesus up through his nineties.

What was his secret for effective, enduring ministry? In his Gospel, rather than identifying himself as "John, the pastor of the church in Jerusalem," or "John, the author of the Revelation," or "John, the apostle," or even simply "John," he used only the simple title, "the disciple whom Jesus loved" (John 13:23; 20:2; 21:20).

Some wonder why John would be so bold as to describe himself that way. But it was not arrogance that motivated him to say that; it was love. John had given his life to his Lord and, in return, received the love of his Lord. He had to proclaim that to others.

Responding to the Love of God

There are two essential ways we can respond to the love of God— the love of the Father through His Son, Jesus:

First, receive God's love

Paul prayed passionately that God would enable the people he served to better comprehend the amazing immensity of the incomprehensible love of God (Ephesians 3:14–21). Open your heart and allow the richness of God's love to heal your brokenness, awaken your deadness, refresh your thirstiness, renew your weariness, fill you with His fullness. When you are struggling, remember that Jesus does love you.

Second, share God's love

John said that we love others because we realize that God loves us (1 John 4:7–10). Take the unconditional, unrelenting love God has given you and pass it on to others. Be the human expression of God's love to them.

Big Thought:

God loves with an invincible, undeniable, sacrificial, selfless, redemptive love. Receive it and share it.

Quote to Ponder

"Found guilty of an excess of love," our Savior was put to death that he might redeem us. He could lose his life for us, but he could not lose his love to us. O mighty force!
Charles H. Spurgeon[2]

Questions to Consider

1. In this study, what big truth about the love of God caught your attention?
2. What area of your life needs to be touched by the love of God?

DAY
25

KNOWING GOD BY HIS ATTRIBUTES:
THE GOODNESS OF GOD

God Is Righteous and Just

One of my favorite types of story features the good guy winning in the end and the bad guy getting what's coming to him. In literature, this is called *poetic justice*: good characters are rewarded and bad characters are punished, usually by an ironic twist of fate.

The Bible's book of Esther contains a great example of poetic justice. It tells the amazing story of the active, sovereign justice of the Lord God, punishing wrong and rewarding right.

The story opens with the odd happenstance that Esther, a Jew, had been made queen of the powerful Persian king, Xerxes. Soon after, it just so happened that her cousin Mordecai discovered a plot to assassinate the king. Mordecai took action, and the king's life was spared.

Mordecai, however, brought trouble on himself by refusing to bow before the evil prime minister, Haman. So Haman hatched a plot to kill Mordecai and all his fellow Jews.

Hearing of this, Queen Esther put together a plan of her own. First, she called her people to fast and pray. Then she invited the king and Haman to a special banquet.

It just so happened that the night before the banquet, the king was unable to sleep, and he decided to read (of all things) the archival history of his kingdom. Of all the sections he could have read, he just happened to review the one detailing how Mordecai had saved his life. For some reason, Mordecai had never been rewarded for this service.

28 Days to Knowing God — 157

Just then, Haman (of all people) happened to enter the king's court. He was hoping to get permission to hang Mordecai! But before he could ask, the king—thinking of Mordecai's unrewarded heroism—asked Haman how he would honor a man the king wanted to commend. Foolishly assuming the king was talking about him, Haman suggested giving the man a royal robe, a beautiful horse, and a parade in his honor.

The king liked that idea. Then he told Haman to do all of that . . .for *Mordecai!*

So the bad guy had to honor his archenemy, the good guy. I would love to have seen the look on Haman's face. Don't you love the poetic justice?

But there's more.

After the parade, before Haman could try anything else, Queen Esther's servants came to take Haman to the dinner she'd planned.

The king was so delighted with Esther and her banquet that he told her to make any request, which was her plan all along. So she told the king of Haman's plot to kill her and all the Jews in his kingdom. She asked the king to spare them.

Xerxes was enraged by the news. He stepped out, into the garden, to cool down.

The terrified Haman stayed behind to beg Esther for his life. But it just so happened that when the king returned, Haman was near Esther's couch, awkwardly pleading his case. The king quickly assumed Haman had tried to sexually assault her and became even more angry. Now, a servant pointed out the gallows that Haman had just happened to have built to kill Mordecai.

So the bad guy, who tried to kill the good guys, was hung on the very gallows he had built. Don't you love the poetic justice?

But there is even more.

The king gave Haman's estate to Esther and Haman's position and signet ring to Mordecai. With that ring, Mordecai had the authority to cancel the previous order and spare the life of all the Jews. He could also give the Jews the right to kill and plunder anyone who tried to attack them.

Let's recap: The bad guy had to honor the good guy and was

hung on the very gallows he had prepared for the good guy. And the good guys got richly rewarded with the bad guy's stuff.

That is poetic justice at its best.

We love these types of stories because we are made in the image of a just God. We also love these stories because they remind us that, one day, God will make everything right. And if not in this life, then definitely in the next.

God Is Just

When we say that God is just, we are stating that He always is and always does right. He is always correct, true, good, virtuous, moral, holy, and pure. He acts without guilt, sin, or corruption. Just and righteous is what God is, and what He does is just and righteous.

The terms *righteous* and *just* are used interchangeably in the Bible, often in describing God.

Righteousness and justice are the foundation of your throne.
PSALM 89:14

He is the Rock, his works are perfect, and all his ways are just. A faithful God who does no wrong, upright and just is he.
DEUTERONOMY 32:4

The LORD is a God of justice.
ISAIAH 30:18

"It is unthinkable that God would do wrong, that the Almighty would pervert justice."
JOB 34:12

The strength of the King loves justice and righteous judgment; You have established fairness; You have executed justice and righteousness in Jacob (Israel).
PSALM 99:4 AMP

*"There is no God apart from me, a righteous God
and a Savior; there is none but me."*
ISAIAH 45:21

*"With the LORD our God there is no injustice
or partiality or bribery."*
2 CHRONICLES 19:7

God Acts Justly

Because God is just, all of His deeds are just. As He governs the earth, He acts justly on behalf of the downtrodden. He can be counted on to respond properly to both the righteous and the wicked.

The LORD works righteousness and justice for all the oppressed.
PSALM 103:6

*He upholds the cause of the oppressed and gives food to the
hungry. The LORD sets prisoners free, the LORD gives sight to
the blind, the LORD lifts up those who are bowed down,
the LORD loves the righteous. The LORD watches over the
foreigner and sustains the fatherless and the widow,
but he frustrates the ways of the wicked.*
PSALM 146:7–9

*Oh, let the nations be glad and sing for joy! For You shall judge
the people righteously, and govern the nations on earth.*
PSALM 67:4 NKJV

*The Almighty is beyond our reach and exalted in power; in his
justice and great righteousness, he does not oppress.*
JOB 37:23

God Will Judge, and Will Judge Justly

Justice is not a passive quality. It calls for action. It demands that injustice be judged and punished, and God is the ultimate judge of all who are in the universe. The apostle Paul referred to God as "the Lord, the righteous Judge" (2 Timothy 4:8). The author of Hebrews called Him "God, the Judge of all" (Hebrews 12:23). James said the Lord is the only one who qualifies as "Lawgiver and Judge" (James 4:12) and called Him "The Judge" (James 5:9). Abraham called God "the Judge of all the earth" (Genesis 18:25), and the psalmist, "Judge of the earth" (Psalm 94:2).

No one will ever be mistreated or misjudged at God's throne, as His judgment will be righteous and just (Psalm 9:8; 96:13; 98:9). One day, there will be a great outpouring of justice as "justice roll[s] on like a river, righteousness like a never-failing stream" (Amos 5:24).

God's judgment will be universal. No one will escape it.

"I will judge each of you according to your own ways."
EZEKIEL 33:20

People are destined to die once, and after
that to face judgment.
HEBREWS 9:27

Each of us will give an account of ourselves to God.
ROMANS 14:12

For believers, this judgment will be an evaluation (and celebration) in which Jesus rewards Christians for their service.

For we must all appear before the judgment seat of Christ,
so that each of us may receive what is due us for the
things done while in the body, whether good or bad.
2 CORINTHIANS 5:10, SEE ALSO PSALM 58:11

If anyone builds on this foundation using gold, silver, costly
stones, wood, hay or straw, their work will be shown for what it
is, because the Day will bring it to light. It will be revealed with
fire, and the fire will test the quality of each person's work. If
what has been built survives, the builder will receive a reward.
1 CORINTHIANS 3:12–14

For nonbelievers, final judgment will occur at the "great white throne." This comprehensive judgment will not result in reward, but punishment.

> Then I saw a great white throne and him who was seated on it. The earth and the heavens fled from his presence, and there was no place for them. And I saw the dead, great and small, standing before the throne, and books were opened. Another book was opened, which is the book of life. The dead were judged according to what they had done as recorded in the books. . . . Anyone whose name was not found written in the book of life was thrown into the lake of fire.
> REVELATION 20:11–12, 15

The Portrait of Perfect Justice

Because of His absolute holiness, God hates sin. Because of His justice, He must judge and punish sin. That puts each of us in a terrible bind—our sin has created an impenetrable barrier between us and God. Our sin bought us a perfectly just decree of "guilty," and a just punishment of death and separation from God (Romans 6:23).

But God is also perfectly merciful. He longs to withhold punishment. He is gracious and longs to give blessings. Yet justice has to be served.

Since He is perfectly wise, God devised the perfect solution. He became one of us, living a sinless life on earth. In His absolute innocence, Jesus deserved life and union with the Father. Yet, in order to satisfy justice, Jesus took our sin upon Himself, accepting our penalty and punishment. He died in our place. Then, to prove that justice was appeased, He rose from the dead.

> God made him who had no sin to be sin for us, so that in him we might become the righteousness of God.
> 2 CORINTHIANS 5:21

> For Christ also suffered once for sins, the righteous for the unrighteous, to bring you to God. He was put to death

in the body but made alive in the Spirit.
1 PETER 3:18

Responding to the Justice of God

Because of what God has done for us through Jesus, we don't need to respond to His justice with fear and trembling. If we trust Jesus as Lord and turn from our sin, we can live in gratitude for God's plan of salvation—for the work of Jesus in dying for our sin.

We also need not live in frustration at the injustices that riddle our world. Knowing that God is just gives us confidence that He will ultimately make everything right.

And, finally, knowing that all will be judged should motivate us to share the love of God with others.

BIG THOUGHT:

God is just. We can receive His just payment for our sins—Jesus—and be saved *and* we can rejoice that all injustice will one day be made right.

Quote to Ponder

At the end of time, the Lord will right all the wrongs of the ages, and even the people most deprived and mistreated in this life will be satisfied with God's justice. Ultimately, no one will have reason to accuse Him of being unfair.
HERBERT VANDER LUGT[1]

Questions to Consider

1. Where in your life do you want to see the justice of God at work?
2. Which appeals to you more—the just work of God in sending Jesus to die for your sins, or the confident hope that one day, the just God will right every wrong? Why?

DAY
26

KNOWING GOD BY HIS ATTRIBUTES:
THE GOODNESS OF GOD

God Is Merciful and Gracious

Jesus had been taken by Jewish authorities on Thursday evening. He was paraded through a series of unjust trials, falsely accused and falsely convicted. He had been brutally beaten and whipped to the point of death. A cruel crown of thorns was placed on His head. Roman soldiers had punched and mocked Him. They made Him carry His cross up the hill called Golgotha ("the Skull"). And now He was being crucified between two criminals. The crowd was scorning Him. An innocent man was being tortured to death and the city had come out to watch.

You would think the first words out of Jesus' mouth would be righteous indignation at the Jewish leaders for orchestrating this awful scene. Or possibly rage at the Romans for carrying out the execution. Or contempt toward the crowd for turning on Him.

Maybe Jesus would utter a defense of His innocence or a description of His many good deeds. Maybe He would call into question the people's sanity or system of justice. How could they possibly kill an innocent man, especially when He is the Son of God!

Maybe He would cry for pity and beg for help. Perhaps He'd take back those comments about being the Son of God. Maybe He would renounce the belief in His own divinity. Something, anything, to end this nightmare.

Or, possibly, Jesus—the King of kings and Lord of lords—would call the heavenly host to take Him down off this inhuman tool of execution. He would shout the order for a thousand angels to swoop down and murder this ungodly mob, the brutal Roman soldiers, and the treacherous Jewish leaders.

No.

The first words out of Jesus' mouth that fateful day in Jerusalem were not words of anger or hurt or fear. He did not say, "Crush them," "Punish them," or "Kill them." He did not command angels to set Him free. He spoke words of mercy.

> *"Father, forgive them, for they do not*
> *know what they are doing."*
> Luke 23:34

Guilt and Forgiveness

We all battle guilt feelings occasionally, and some of us wrestle with them daily. True guilt is an objective fact based on a specific reality—it is the condition of being separated from God and deserving judgment because of sin. Depending on what we do with it, true guilt can be beneficial or detrimental. It can drive us to God for forgiveness. Or we might push the feeling deep into our subconscious.

Guilt often produces anxiety, fear, worry, pessimism, a critical spirit, and feelings of inferiority. It can poison our relationships by producing anger, criticism, bitterness, insults, and accusations. Unresolved guilt can even cause physical illness, alcoholism or drug abuse, under- or overeating, overwork or lack of productivity, criminal activity, gambling, frigidity or impotence, masochism or sadism, or a controlling and manipulative personality. Truly, no emotion is more destructive than guilt.

But forgiveness counteracts every effect of guilt. The word *forgive* speaks of pardoning an offense, canceling a debt, removing guilt, and relieving payment. Jesus knew that what we need is forgiveness.

Guilt is a weight. I remember times in my life when I felt the burden, like a bag of bricks slung over my shoulders.

Forgiveness is the removal of this weight.

Guilt is a cancer that, if allowed to continue, will grow and spread. It eventually kills whatever it touches.

Guilt is a debt that is beyond our ability to pay. It is huge and suffocating.

Forgiveness is the complete canceling of that overwhelming debt.

Guilt is a jail that imprisons our soul.

Forgiveness is the key that sets us free.

Guilt is like a sentence of death that hangs over our head, robbing us of joy and life.

Forgiveness is the pardon that clears our name forever.

Guilt is like a wall that separates us from really relating to others.

Forgiveness opens a door in the wall. Better still, it is like a crane that knocks the wall down—or even a bomb that blows the wall up.

"Father, Forgive Them"

With those three simple words Jesus decreed a moratorium on guilt. The ironic beauty of these words is not that they *were* spoken, but rather in *who* spoke them, and where He was when He did.

"Father, forgive them" was spoken by Jesus, the Son of God, the only sinless person who ever lived. The only person in history who never needed to be forgiven.

Jesus spoke those words on the cross, the place of His death. He didn't deserve death. Yet there He was, dying to pay for *our* sins, so *we* could be forgiven. He allowed Himself to be arrested by a band of corrupt temple guards. He allowed Himself to be unjustly accused and tried. He allowed Himself to be wrongly condemned. He allowed Himself to be crucified.

Why?

So the wall of separation between God and us could be torn down.

So our sin debt could be paid in full.

So the weight of guilt could be lifted from our backs.

So we could receive a full pardon from the Lord of the universe.

So we could be forgiven.

The Mercy of God

What is the mercy of God? It is the withholding of the judgment we deserve because Jesus took our judgment upon Himself. Mercy is God not exacting the penalty for our sin because Jesus paid the penalty for us.

How can we receive God's mercy? We need to confess our sin.

If we confess our sins, he is faithful and just and will forgive us our sins and purify us from all unrighteousness.
1 JOHN 1:9

Whoever conceals their sins does not prosper, but the one who confesses and renounces them finds mercy.
PROVERBS 28:13

Confess means literally "to say the same thing." Confession is acknowledging our sin and agreeing with God that it is wrong. It means to agree that God's standard is just—and that we have either broken it or fallen short of it.

Confession is accepting responsibility for our sins, and it is the key that unlocks the door of forgiveness. True confession leads to a clear conscience, which heals our guilty soul. A clear conscience is one in which all aspects of guilt have been removed through confession.

How do we find freedom from guilt? Accept God's forgiveness. When we confess our sin, God forgives, removes, hides, sweeps away, and pardons it. He tramples it under His feet. And then He remembers it no more!

You forgave the iniquity of your people and covered all their sins.
PSALM 85:2

As far as the east is from the west, so far has he removed our transgressions from us.
PSALM 103:12

You have put all my sins behind your back.
ISAIAH 38:17

"I have swept away your offenses like a cloud,
your sins like the morning mist."
ISAIAH 44:22

Who is a God like you, who pardons sin and forgives
the transgression of the remnant of his inheritance?
You do not stay angry forever but delight to show
mercy. You will again have compassion on us;
you will tread our sins underfoot and hurl all
our iniquities into the depths of the sea.
MICAH 7:18–19

"I will forgive their wickedness and will
remember their sins no more."
JEREMIAH 31:34

The Portrait of Grace

Jesus was not the only one crucified on Golgotha that fateful day. Two thieves were hanging on either side of Him.

Then one of the criminals who were hanged blasphemed Him, saying, "If You are the Christ, save Yourself and us."
But the other, answering, rebuked him, saying, "Do you not even fear God, seeing you are under the same condemnation? And we indeed justly, for we receive the due reward of our deeds; but this Man has done nothing wrong."
Then he said to Jesus, "Lord, remember me when You come into Your kingdom."
And Jesus said to him, "Assuredly, I say to you, today you will be with Me in Paradise."
LUKE 23:39–43 NKJV

This scene reminds us that it's possible to be right next to Jesus and still miss His mercy and grace. One thief hung just a few feet from the Son of God and missed forgiveness, but the other thief *was* changed—and will be waiting in Paradise to tell us all about it.

Today you will be with Me in Paradise

The thief, dying on a cross beside Jesus, had done nothing to warrant help from God. He was a criminal—deemed by society to be worthy of the most vulgar, painful death. At first, along with the others, he had mocked Jesus. What right did *he* have to receive God's mercy and grace?

Do you really want to know?

The thief had the same right that you and I have to salvation. We are all just like him—sinful, guilty, helpless, desperate. We have done nothing to merit or earn salvation. Instead, just as the thief did, we receive salvation as a gift. This is the grace of God

It is by grace you have been saved, through faith—
and this not from yourselves, it is the gift of God—
not by works, so that no one can boast.
Ephesians 2:8–9

The Grace of God

What is the grace of God? It is God giving us blessings we do not deserve and did not earn. It is God favoring us with unmerited benefits.

The *justice* of God is the righteous demand that He punish us for our sins.

The *love* of God is Jesus taking our place to die for our sins.

The *mercy* of God is His not giving us the great punishment we deserve.

The *grace* of God is His giving us great blessing that we do *not* deserve.

On the cross, the justice of God was satisfied. Then Jesus could extend to us the amazing grace and mercy of God.

Responding to the Grace and Mercy of God

We show our appreciation for God's grace and mercy by being gracious and merciful to others. You may think, *But they do not deserve it*. Of course not. Neither did you or I. God's grace and mercy are gifts that we humbly receive and graciously give, even to the undeserving.

BIG THOUGHT:

God withholds the judgment we deserve and gives us blessings we don't. We must learn to treat others the same way.

Quote to Ponder

> *Amazing grace! (how sweet the sound)*
> *That saved a wretch like me!*
> *I once was lost, but now am found,*
> *Was blind, but now I see.*
> JOHN NEWTON[1]

Questions to Consider

1. What does the cross teach you about God's grace and mercy?
2. How well do you extend grace and mercy to others?

KNOWING GOD BY HIS ATTRIBUTES:
THE GOODNESS OF GOD

God Is Faithful

Life is difficult. But God is faithful.
People are unreliable. But God is faithful.
We don't know the future. But God is faithful.
We need help. But God is faithful.
Trust Him!

The Faithfulness of God

Faithfulness speaks of that which is steadfast, loyal, solid, firm, and constant. It refers to one who is dependable, who keeps his promises, and whose actions match his words. Because of God's faithfulness, He is a trustworthy object of hope, a steadfast basis of trust, a firm foundation of faith, and a constant source of comfort.

Faithfulness is an attribute of God. It results from His acting in a manner that is always consistent with His other attributes. Faithfulness is not something God *does*; it is simply who He *is*.

God's faithfulness is our shield (Psalm 91:4), and it extends to all generations (Psalm 100:5). God remains faithful forever (Psalm 146:6). He carries out His plans with absolute faithfulness (Isaiah 25:1). His faithfulness guarantees the fulfillment of His promises (2 Corinthians 1:20).

In the wilderness, Moses encouraged the Hebrews with the fact that God would keep His promises to them. It would have nothing to do with *them* and everything to do with *Him*. God would be faithful because God *is* faithful.

> *The LORD did not set his affection on you and choose you
> because you were more numerous than other peoples,
> for you were the fewest of all peoples. But it was because
> the LORD loved you and kept the oath he swore to your
> ancestors that he brought you out with a mighty hand
> and redeemed you from the land of slavery, from the
> power of Pharaoh king of Egypt. Know therefore that
> the LORD your God is God; he is the faithful God,
> keeping his covenant of love to a thousand generations
> of those who love him and keep his commandments.*
> DEUTERONOMY 7:7–9

God is faithful. Trust Him.

GOD IS TRUE

God's very being is true. All of God's actions conform with truth, and all truth conforms with God. There is nothing false or insincere in His being. Everything about Him confirms and defines reality.

God, by His very nature *is* truth (John 14:6). He is called "the God of truth" (Isaiah 65:16 NKJV), He abounds in truth (Exodus 34:6 AMP), He speaks the truth (Psalm 19:9; John 17:17), and He makes judgments with truth (Revelation 16:7).

God has never lied, nor will He, or even could He. His proclamations and promises are all real, reliable, actual, and accurate.

> *"God is not human, that he should lie, not a human being,
> that he should change his mind. Does he speak and
> then not act? Does he promise and not fulfill?"*
> NUMBERS 23:19

God is true. He is faithful. Trust Him.

GOD DOES NOT CHANGE

God is immutable. He is not subject to change through time or circumstance. His essence, nature, or character will not change (Psalm 102:26-27). God never becomes less truthful or merciful or just or good than He has ever been before. He is always the same. In no way does God ever diminish—He is, in every way, indestructible (Hebrews 7:16). God is immortal (Romans 1:23).

The Lord always has been and always will be all that He is . . .and exactly as He is. He is eternal, immutable, immortal, and perfect. God has not changed, does not change, and will not change. He declared through the prophet Malachi, "I the LORD do not change" (Malachi 3:6). James described God as "the Father of the heavenly lights, who does not change like shifting shadows" (James 1:17). The author of Hebrews stated, "Jesus Christ is the same yesterday and today and forever" (Hebrews 13:8). When Moses asked God for His name, the Lord responded, "I AM WHO I AM" (Exodus 3:14).

Moses had concluded his life and ministry—at the edge of the Promised land—with a song. In it he compared the changeless faithfulness of God to unyielding stone.

He is the Rock, his works are perfect, and all his ways are just.
A faithful God who does no wrong, upright and just is he.
DEUTERONOMY 32:4

Speaking to God, the psalmist declared that the heavens and earth "will perish, but you remain; they will all wear out like a garment. Like clothing you will change them and they will be discarded. But you remain the same, and your years will never end" (Psalm 102:26-27).

God is immutable, everlasting, incorruptible, immortal, unchanging. Therefore, God is completely and constantly faithful. Trust Him.

GOD IS ETERNAL

As we discussed on day 17, God is the eternal King (Jeremiah 10:10). He is free from the tyranny of time. In God there is no past or future—He dwells in a never-ending present. He is enthroned forever and His fame endures through all generations

(Psalm 102:12). He has been, is, and will be God "from everlasting to everlasting" (Psalm 90:2).

God is eternally faithful. You can trust Him.

God Is Faithful

Because faithfulness is who God is, everything He does is done in faithfulness—including the great promises He makes. A promise is meaningless unless the person making that promise can and will keep it. Repeatedly, scripture declares that God is faithful to keep His promises according to the principles of His Word (Psalm 119:86, 138; Deuteronomy 7:9; Isaiah 49:7; 55:3; 1 Corinthians 1:8–9).

Here is a sampling of the great promises of God's faithfulness.

If we are faithless, he remains faithful,
for he cannot disown himself.
2 TIMOTHY 2:13

Your love, LORD, reaches to the heavens,
your faithfulness to the skies.
PSALM 36:5

I will declare that your love stands firm forever, that
you have established your faithfulness in heaven itself.
PSALM 89:2

"The grass withers and the flowers fall,
but the word of our God endures forever."
ISAIAH 40:8

Let us hold unswervingly to the hope we profess,
for he who promised is faithful.
HEBREWS 10:23

If we confess our sins, he is faithful and just and will forgive
us our sins and purify us from all unrighteousness.
1 JOHN 1:9

No temptation has overtaken you except what is common to mankind. And God is faithful; he will not let you be tempted beyond what you can bear. But when you are tempted, he will also provide a way out so that you can endure it.
1 Corinthians 10:13

Lord, hear my prayer, listen to my cry for mercy; in your faithfulness and righteousness come to my relief.
Psalm 143:1

The Lord is faithful, and he will strengthen you and protect you from the evil one.
2 Thessalonians 3:3

God is faithful. Trust Him.

God's Faithfulness Is the Source of Hope

The Old Testament book of Lamentations lives up to its name. In it, the prophet Jeremiah mourns the demolition and devastation of the once glorious city of Jerusalem. He decries the disobedience that led to Jerusalem's defeat and downfall. In passionate, poetic language he portrays the extent of sorrow from every conceivable vantage point.

Depleted, deflated, and deeply depressed, Jeremiah has only one thin thread of hope—the faithfulness of God.

I remember my affliction and my wandering, the bitterness and the gall. I well remember them, and my soul is downcast within me. Yet this I call to mind and therefore I have hope: Because of the Lord's great love we are not consumed, for his compassions never fail. They are new every morning; great is your faithfulness.
Lamentations 3:19–23

I have never experienced the devastation Jeremiah endured some twenty-six hundred years ago in Jerusalem. But I have felt overwhelmingly emptied, desolated, and crushed. Life can be hard—brutally unfair and unkind. Many times, I have found assurance in Jeremiah's promise of the faithfulness of God.

Eventually, all of us discover that there is nothing in this world we can always rely on. The weather changes. Business has downturns. People break their promises. Parents age and die.

But there is one thing—and only one thing—that we can rely on. *God* is absolutely, always fully dependable. He will always keep His promises. His actions always match His words and character perfectly. God is faithful. And because of this, He is a trustworthy object of hope, a steadfast basis of trust, a firm foundation for faith, and a constant source of comfort.

Responding to the Faithfulness of God

There are two logical responses to the faithfulness of God. The first is to trust Him. The second is to strive to imitate Him. How? By keeping our own word, always doing our part, and showing loyalty to Him and His people.

BIG THOUGHT:

Everything about God speaks of His faithfulness. This gives us unshakable hope.

Quote

God's strength behind you, His concern for you, His love within you, and His arms beneath you are more than sufficient for the job ahead of you.
WILLIAM ARTHUR WARD[1]

Questions

1. How does God's immutability, truth, and eternality contribute to His faithfulness?
2. What aspect of God's faithfulness do you find most encouraging?

BRINGING IT ALL TOGETHER

God Is Worthy of Worship

Several years ago, in a Turkish street café, I was having coffee with a Christian worker. This longtime missionary to Muslims was severely shaken as two of his colleagues had been martyred just a few months earlier. Their families were crushed by grief.

My friend and his own family had been rudely booted from the country several times during an escalating oppression of Christians. It hurt him to see his own wife and children suffer.

He looked me in the eye and asked, "Is it worth it?"

"What you are really asking is this: Is God worth it?" I responded. "Is He worth suffering for? Is He worth dying for?" I paused, then said, "You know the answer to that question."

God Is Worthy

Our English word *worship* comes from the concept "worth-ship." The idea is simply that God is "worth it." Therefore, worship is a response to God's worth.

We all have a longing to live for something larger than ourselves. There is an inner urge to surrender to something more powerful, more majestic, more beautiful than we ourselves are. God has etched into our hearts a cry for the eternal. He created us with a yearning to *worship*.

These longings of our heart are met in the person of God. He deserves our worship.

"You Are Worthy"

Two thousand years ago, the Spirit of the Lord gave John a vision.

He saw a coming day around the throne of God, an enormous throne stretching to such a height that he shrank before it. Encircling the throne was the most amazing array of color possible. A series of seven fires danced in ascending, then descending steps before the throne, the smoke of their flames rising rhythmically to an unknown beat.

If the sights were not enough to leave John openmouthed and gasping in awe, the sounds were. Immense rumblings exploded as lightning ripped through the sky. Thunder roared, shaking the poor old man's bones.

Anchoring the four corners of the throne were giant angelic beings. Each was an oddly glorious symphony of wings, eyes, color, light, and beautiful antiphonal praise as they chanted, "'Holy, holy, holy, is the Lord God Almighty', who was, and is, and is to come" (Revelation 4:8).

John noticed others around the throne too—wise men, elders, church leaders, saints. All were wearing pure white robes and a golden crown. Each was stretched out facedown before the throne, crushed and intoxicated by the mountainous, majestic, magnificent glory of the amazing One who sat on the throne. In an act of worship, they cast their crowns at the feet of the Worthy One.

> The twenty-four elders fall down before Him who sits on the throne and worship Him who lives forever and ever, and cast their crowns before the throne, saying: "You are worthy, O Lord, to receive glory and honor and power; for You created all things, and by Your will they exist and were created."
> REVELATION 4:10–11, NKJV

Then the scene shifted from the Father to the Son. An angel asked, "Who is worthy?" (Revelation 5:2). A litany of beings was declared to be unworthy, but the angel identified One who is indeed worthy: "the Lion of the tribe of Judah" (Revelation 5:5).

Perhaps John expected to see a proud warrior king, chest adorned with medals of honor, courage, and bravery. But what he saw stunned him. At center stage, surrounded by angels and elders, was not a powerful lion—it was "a Lamb as though it had been slain" (Revelation 5:6 NKJV).

Then the angels, the elders, and every person who ever lived declared the worthiness of the lion, the lamb, King Jesus!

> *"You are worthy to take the scroll, and to open its seals;*
> *for You were slain, and have redeemed us to God by Your*
> *blood out of every tribe and tongue and people and*
> *nation, and have made us kings and priests to our God;*
> *and we shall reign on the earth."*
> REVELATION 5:9–10, NKJV

He is worthy of worship.

Worthy of Worship, No Matter What

It was the worst day of Job's life. He was sucker-punched and smothered by sorrow as one messenger after another brought him increasingly horrendous news. In a matter of hours, Job's fortune, business, career, property, employees, and retirement had all been viciously jerked from his hands. They were all gone.

But the last message of the day made that massive loss seem inconsequential: all ten of his children had been killed.

It would be devastating to lose one child, let alone all of your kids at once. Satan was doing all he could to cause Job to curse God (Job 1:9–11).

What Job did next is a testimony to his knowledge of God. Interestingly, he did not have the whole Bible available to him—in fact, many believe that Job's story was one of the first books written. Yet his actions indicated that he obviously knew and appreciated God. What did he do? Job declared that God was worth it, no matter what.

> *At this, Job got up and tore his robe and shaved his head. Then*
> *he fell to the ground in worship and said: "Naked I came from*
> *my mother's womb, and naked I will depart. The LORD gave and*
> *the LORD has taken away; may the name of the LORD be praised."*
> JOB 1:20–21

Worthy of Worship, No Matter the Price

Finally, everything seemed to be going well for Abraham. After years of waiting, the impossible had occurred: he and his aged wife, Sarah, finally had a son.

The miracle-born boy was named *Isaac*, meaning "laughter." In years to come, the boy would marry and have his own children—and God's promise that Abraham would father a nation could begin to be fulfilled.

But then God asked Abraham to do the unthinkable. As it is recorded in Genesis,

> *Some time later God tested Abraham. He said to him,*
> *"Abraham!" "Here I am," he replied. Then God said,*
> *"Take your son, your only son, whom you love—Isaac—*
> *and go to the region of Moriah. Sacrifice him there*
> *as a burnt offering on a mountain I will show you."*
> GENESIS 22:1–2

Wait a minute! God told Abraham to take his dearest possession, his miracle son, the son of the promise, Isaac, and *sacrifice* him? This would be the ultimate test of obedience.

A "god" is anything to which we devote our time, attention, and energy. It is the one thing that takes priority over all the other things. I imagine it would have been easy for Abraham to make Isaac his god.

And I am sure that Abraham would have gladly given God everything else in his life. . .including his own life itself. But not this—not his miracle son, the one on whom rested the entirety of God's promises to Abraham. Isaac was the only off-limits, untouchable, non-negotiable area of Abraham's life.

But, of course, God knew that.

This deep fatherly love for Isaac was the only thing that could ever stand between Abraham and God. So Isaac is what God asked for.

As I think about this story, the audacity of the request stuns me. But it is Abraham's response that blows my mind and puts me on my knees.

*Early the next morning Abraham got up and loaded his
donkey. He took with him two of his servants and his son
Isaac. When he had cut enough wood for the burnt offering,
he set out for the place God had told him about.*
GENESIS 22:3

Notice there is no mention of Abraham arguing with God, complaining to God, or bargaining with God. None. "Early the next morning" he got up and *obeyed God*. But even that is not the most amazing part of this story.

*On the third day Abraham looked up and saw the place
in the distance. He said to his servants, "Stay here
with the donkey while I and the boy go over there.
We will worship and then we will come back to you."*
GENESIS 22:4–5

"We will worship."

Soon, Abraham was raising his knife to sacrifice his dearly loved son to his even more dearly loved God. And, stunningly, Isaac went along. But they did not see this as a sacrifice—to them, it was worship. For Abraham and Isaac, worshipping meant obeying God no matter how high the price or personal the loss.

God honored their obedience, and stopped Abraham before Isaac was killed.

People who know God know that He is worthy of worship.

Worthy of Worship, Every Day

One of my favorite devotional authors is A. W. Tozer, a busy, self-taught pastor and author who wonderfully combined truth and fire. He had a God-given ability to challenge the mind and cut to the heart. Tozer was especially passionate about worship.

One thing he emphasized was that God deserved to be worshipped more than one day a week. Tozer said, "If we are so engaged in our Saturday pursuits that we are far from His presence and far from a sense of worship on Saturday, we are not in very good shape to worship Him on Sunday."[1] He also said, "If you cannot worship the Lord in the midst of your responsibilities on Monday, it is not likely that you were worshiping on Sunday!"[2]

A Challenge

I trust that this twenty-eight-day study of God has accomplished significant things in your life. My desire is that you have stretched your view of God, deepened your faith in Him, intensified your passion for Him, and strengthened your relationship with Him.

I especially hope that everything you have learned about God has driven the conviction in your heart that He is worthy of absolute, unshakable, daily no-matter-the-price worship. Now I want to challenge you: use what you have learned as a foundation to build a life of everyday worship.

Note that none of the examples in this chapter had anything to do with music. How do you worship God without song?

- Praise Him for some of His names or attributes each day.
- Surrender yourself to Him each day. Be specific. Name aspects of your life, one by one, as you dedicate them to God. Give God your "Isaacs."
- Look around—see all the ways God is working in your life, and thank Him for them.
- Take daily inventory of your life, and cast down any false gods.

God is the only one who is perfectly, perpetually, and infinitely great, eternal, present, majestic, and sovereign. He alone is holy, loving, righteous, merciful, gracious, trustworthy, and faithful. Only God can call Himself *YHWH* (The Great I AM), *El Shaddai* (Almighty God), *El Elyon* (God Most High), and *Adonai* (Lord and Master). He is all we will ever need *and* so much more.

Worship Him!

BIG THOUGHT:

God is worthy of absolute, unshakable, daily, no-matter-the-price worship. Learn to live a life of worship.

Quote to Ponder

I would rather worship God than do any other thing I know of in all this wide world.
A. W. Tozer[3]

Questions to Consider

1. What did you learn about God or worship from this chapter?
2. How will you respond to the call to live the life of a worshipper?
3. Name three big truths about God that you needed as you studied this book.

Suggestions for Small Groups

I love small groups!

I have been leading small groups for forty years, and I have trained thousands of small group leaders. I am always looking for helpful, simple, biblical, and practical resources.

28 Days to Knowing God is a great resource for small groups. It is full of pertinent scriptures for study—and each chapter concludes with several challenging application questions.

Depending on your group, you could use this book in several ways:

- Study two chapters a week for fourteen weeks.
- Study four chapters a week for seven weeks.
- Study seven chapters a week for four weeks.

For the groups I oversee, I am planning to use the "four chapters a week for seven weeks" plan. May God lead you and your group into a deeper and more passionate knowledge of Himself!

DAVE EARLEY

NOTES

DAY 1

1. J. I. Packer, *Knowing God* (Downers Grove, Illinois: InterVarsity Press, 1973), 36.
2. C. H. Spurgeon, "The Immutability of God," https://www.spurgeon.org/resource-library/sermons/the-immutability-of-god#-flipbook/

DAY 2

1. J. B. Phillips, *Your God Is Too Small* (New York: MacMillan, 1961), 8.

DAY 3

1. Elmer Towns, *My Father's Names* (Ventura, California: Regal Books, 1991), 153.

DAY 4

1. *Star Wars*, produced by Gary Kurtz and directed by George Lucas (20th Century Fox, 1977), motion picture.
2. Hannah Whitall Smith, *The God of All Comfort: The God Who Is Enough* (Chicago: Moody, 1956), 14–15.

DAY 5

1. G. K. Chesterton, *Orthodoxy* (Garden City, New York: Doubleday, 1959), 160.
2. Bruce Marchiano, quoted in Sherwood Wirt, *Jesus Man of Joy* (Eugene, Oregon: Harvest House Publishers, 1999), 9–10.

DAY 6

1. This story is adapted from Rod Dempsey and Dave Earley, *Spiritual Formation Is: Growing in Jesus with Passion and Confidence,* (Nashville, Tennessee: B&H Academic, 2018), 147.
2. Dempsey and Earley, 149.
3. Dempsey and Earley, 149–150.
4. John Ortberg, *The Life You've Always Wanted* (Grand Rapids, Michigan: Zondervan, 1997), 84.

DAY 7

1. A. W. Tozer, *The Pursuit of God* (Harrisburg, Pennsylvania: Christian Publications, Inc., 1948), 5.
2. Martin Luther, quoted in *Martin Luther's Quiet Time* by Walter Trobisch (Carol Stream, Illinois: InterVarsity, 1975), 8.
3. Tozer, *The Divine Conquest* (Harrisburg, Pennsylvania: Christian Publications, Inc., 1950), 5.
4. Billy Graham, *The Journey: How to Live by Faith in an Uncertain World* (Nashville, Tennessee: Thomas Nelson, 2007), 228.

DAY 8

1. Lehman Strauss, *The First Person* (Neptune, New Jersey: Loizeaux Brothers, 1967), 136.

DAY 9

1. Lehman Strauss, *The First Person* (Neptune, New Jersey: Loizeaux Brothers, 1967, 158.
2. Strauss, 159.
3. Charles Swindoll, *Living Beyond the Daily Grind, Book 2: Reflections on the Songs and Sayings in Scripture* (Waco, Texas: W Publishing Group, 1989), 260.
4. Charles Spurgeon, The Treasury of David, "Psalm 91," http://www.romans45.org/spurgeon/treasury/ps091.htm (accessed Oct. 8 2018).

DAY 10

1. Elmer Towns, *My Father's Names* (Ventura, California: Regal Books, 1991), 56.
2. Quoted in Charles Spurgeon, *The Treasury of David, Vol. II,* (Grand Rapids, Michigan, Guardian Press, 1981), 60.

DAY 11

1. Hannah Whitall Smith, *The God of All Comfort* (Chicago: Moody, 1956), 21.
2. Lehman Strauss, *The First Person* (Neptune, New Jersey: Loizeaux Brothers, 1967), 138.

DAY 12

1. Elmer Towns, *My Father's Names* (Ventura, California: Regal books, 1991), 29.
2. C. H. Spurgeon, "The Lord Is My Shepherd," http://www.spurgeongems.org/vols52-54/chs3006.pdf (accessed Sept. 1, 2018).

DAY 13

1. Oswald Chambers, "Our Careful Unbelief," My Utmost for His Highest, https://utmost.org/our-careful-unbelief/ (accessed Sept 1, 2018).

DAY 14

1. Robert Lightner, *The God of the Bible* (Grand Rapids, Michigan: Baker Books, 1975), 116.
2. Samuel Logan Brengle, *Love-Slaves* (Salem, Ohio: Schmul Publishing, 1996), 8.
3. Lehman Strauss, *The First Person*, 154.

DAY 15

1. Augustus Strong, *Systematic Theology* (Rochester, New York: E. R. Andrews,), 255.
2. A. W. Tozer, *The Knowledge of the Holy* (New York: Harper Collins, 1961), 43–44.
3. Strong, 279.
4. Tozer, 23.
5. A. W. Tozer, *Worship: The Missing Jewel* (Camp Hill, Pennsylvania: Christian Publications, Inc., 1992), 21.
6. Corrie ten Boom, Elizabeth Sherrill, and John Sherrill, *The Hiding Place* (Chappaqua, New York: Chosen Books, 1971), 225.

DAY 16

1. Jerry Bridges, *Trusting God Even When Life Hurts* (Colorado Springs, Colorado: NavPress, 2008), 20.
2. Francis Chan, *Crazy Love* (Colorado Springs, Colorado: David C. Cook, 2008), 41.

DAY 17

1. C. S. Lewis quoted in A. W. Tozer, *The Knowledge of the Holy* (New York: HarperCollins, 1961), 45.
2. Tozer, 45.
3. Randy Alcorn, "Why an Eternal Perspective Changes Everything," July 10, 2015, https://www.epm.org/blog/2015/Jul/10/eternal-perspective-changes (accessed June 27, 2018).
4. Joni Erickson Tada, *Heaven: Your Real Home* (Grand Rapids, Michigan: Zondervan, 2018), 152.

DAY 18

1. Lehman Strauss, *The First Person* (Neptune, New Jersey: Loizeaux Brothers, 1967), 67.
2. Allen Fleece, quoted in A. W. Tozer, *The Knowledge of the Holy* (New York: HarperCollins, 1961), 82–83.

DAY 19

1. *American Dictionary of the English Language*, 1828 edition, http://webstersdictionary1828.com/Dictionary/majesty (accessed July 2, 2018).
2. A. W. Tozer, *The Attributes of God* (Camp Hill, Pennsylvania: Wingspread Publishers, 2007), 95.
3. A. W. Tozer, *Success and the Christian* (Chicago: Moody Publishers, 2017), 36.
4. A. W. Pink, "Fearing God in His Sovereign Majesty," The Fear of God, #182, www.chapellibrary.org/files/7313/7643/3203/fog2fg.pdf (accessed Oct. 8, 2018).

DAY 20

1. A. W. Tozer, *Whatever Happened to Worship?* (Camp Hill, Pennsylvania: Wingspread Publishers, 2006), 125.

DAY 21

1. Lehman Strauss, *The First Person* (Neptune, New Jersey: Loizeaux Brothers, 1967), 56.
2. Jerry Bridges, *Trusting God* (Colorado Springs, Colorado: NavPress, 1988), 39.

DAY 22

1. Robert Lightner, *The God of the Bible* (Grand Rapids, Michigan: Baker Book House, 1978), 99.

2. Jerry Bridges, *Trusting God Even When It Hurts* (Colorado Springs, Colorado: NavPress, 1988), 25.

3. A. W. Tozer, *We Travel an Appointed Way* (Camp Hill, Pennsylvania: Wingspread Publishers, 2010), 3.

4. Margaret Clarkson, *Grace Grows Best in Winter* (Grand Rapids, Michigan: Eerdmans, 1984), 40–41.

5. R. C. Sproul, *Essential Truths of the Christian Faith* (Carol Stream, Illinois: Tyndale House, 1998), 62.

DAY 23

1. Lehman Strauss, *The First Person* (Neptune, New Jersey: Loizeaux Brothers, 1967), 80.

2. Jerry Bridges, *The Pursuit of Holiness* (Colorado Springs, Colorado: NavPress, 2006), 10–11.

DAY 24

1. Norma Lee Liles, "The History of 'Jesus Loves Me, This I Know' Song," http://www.inspirationalarchive.com/1730/the-history-of-jesus-loves-me-this-i-know-song/#ixzz5QWmoXqlx (accessed Oct. 22, 2018).

2. Charles H. Spurgeon, "The Secret of Loving God," http://www.biblebb.com/files/spurgeon/2730.htm (accessed Oct. 22, 2018).

DAY 25

1. Herbert Vander Lugt, "Is God Unfair?" https://odb.org/2002/05/07/is-god-unfair/ (accessed Oct. 10, 2018).

DAY 26

1. John Newton, "Amazing Grace," http://www.ccel.org/ccel/newton/olneyhymns.Book1.iCH.h1_41.html?highlight=amazing,grace#highlight (accessed October 22, 2018).

DAY 27

1. William Arthur Ward, quoted in "Ten Awesome Quotes on God's Faithfulness," https://www.godtube.com/news/10-awesome-quotes-about-gods-faithfulness.html (accessed October 12, 2018).

DAY 28
1. A. W. Tozer, *Whatever Happened to Worship?* (Eastbourne, England: Kingsway Publications, 1986), 121–122.
2. Tozer, 122.
3. Tozer, 18.